T0203316

Interoperability for Enterprise Software
and Applications

Interoperability for Enterprise Software and Applications

*Proceedings of the Workshops and the Doctorial Symposium
of the I-ESA International Conference 2010*

Edited by
Hervé Panetto
Nacer Boudjlida

Library of Congress Cataloging-in-Publication Data

International Conference on Interoperability of Enterprise Software and Applications (6th : 2010 : Coventry, England)
Interoperability for enterprise software and applications : proceedings of the workshops and the doctorial symposium of the I-ESA International Conference 2010 / edited by Hervé Panetto, Nacer Boudjlida.
p. cm.
Includes bibliographical references and index.
ISBN 978-1-84821-270-1
1. Internetworking (Telecommunication)--Congresses. I. Panetto, Hervé. II. Boudjlida, Nacer. III. Title.
TK5105.5.I57155 2010
004.6--dc20

2010022202

British Library Cataloguing-in-Publication Data
A CIP record for this book is available from the British Library
ISBN 978-1-84821-270-1

Printed and bound in Great Britain by CPI Antony Rowe, Chippenham and Eastbourne.

Sixth International Conference
I-ESA'2010
Interoperability for Enterprise Software and Applications

Coventry, United Kingdom, April 12th – 15th, 2010

Supported by INTEROP-VLab

Interoperability in enterprise applications can be defined as the ability of a system or a product to work with other systems or products without special effort from the customer or user. The possibility of interacting and exchanging information with internal and external collaborators is a key issue in the enterprise sector. It is fundamental in order to produce goods and services quickly, at lower cost, while maintaining higher levels of quality and customization. Interoperability is considered to be achieved if the interaction can, at least, take place at three levels: data, applications and business enterprise through the architecture of the enterprise model and taking into account the semantics. It is not only a problem of software and IT technologies. It involves support for communication and transactions between different organizations that must be based on shared business references.

The I-ESA conference aimed at bringing together research, users and practitioners dealing with different issues of Interoperability for Enterprise Software and Applications. The conference focused on interoperability-related research areas ranging from *Enterprise Modeling* to define interoperability requirements, *Architecture and Platforms* to provide implementation frameworks and *Ontologies* to define interoperability semantics in the enterprise.

General Co-Chairs
Keith Popplewell, Coventry University, UK
Jenny Harding, Loughborough University, UK

Conference Program Co-Chairs
Raul Poler, Polytechnic University of Valencia, Spain
Ricardo Chalmeta, University of Jaume I, Spain

Workshop Co-Chairs
Nacer Boudjlida, LORIA UMR 7503, Nancy University, France
Hervé Panetto, CRAN UMR 7039, Nancy University, France

Doctoral Symposium Chair
Jenny Harding, Loughborough University, UK

Workshop Organizers

Standards – A Foundation for Interoperability
Martin Zelm, CIMOSA Association, Germany
David Chen, University of Bordeaux, France

Use of MDI/SOA Concepts in Industry
Guy Doumeingts, GFI, France
Martine Grandin-Dubost, GFI, France

Dynamic Management across Interoperating Enterprises
Colin Piddington, Cimmedia, UK
Georgios Kapogiannis, Think Lab, University of Salford, UK

I-ESA Workshops Committees

General Workshop Chairs

Hervé Panetto, CRAN UMR 7039, Nancy University, CNRS, France
Nacer Boudjlida, LORIA UMR 7503, Nancy University, CNRS, France

Standards – A Foundation for Interoperability
Workshop Chairs

Martin Zelm, CIMOSA Association, Germany
David Chen, University of Bordeaux, France

Workshop Program Committee

Piero De Sabbata, ENEA, Italy
Ricardo Goncalves, Uninova, Portugal
Kurt Kosanke, CIMOSA Association, Germany
David Shorter, IT FOCUS, UK

Use of MDI/SOA Concepts in Industry
Workshop Chairs

Guy Doumeingts, GFI, France
Martine Grandin-Dubost, GFI, France

Workshop Program Committee

Pontus Johnson, KTH, Sweden
Stephan Kassel, University of Applied Sciences Zwickau, Germany
Hervé Pingaud, EMAC Albi, France

Dynamic Management across Interoperating Enterprises
Workshop Chairs

Colin Piddington, Cimmedia, UK
Georgios Kapogiannis, Think Lab, University of Salford, UK

Workshop Program Committee

Martin Zelm, Cimosa, Germany
Frank-Walter Jaekel, IPK, Germany
Professor Lauri Koskela, University of Salford, UK

Doctoral Symposium
Workshop Chair

Jenny A. Harding, Loughborough University, UK

Doctoral Symposium Reviewing Committee

Keith Popplewell, Coventry University, UK
Alok Choudhary, Loughborough University, UK
Claire Palmer, Loughborough University, UK

Table of Contents

Editorial

The Sixth I-ESA International Conference (13-15 April 2010, Coventry, UK), supported by the INTEROP VLab (International Virtual Laboratory on Enterprise Interoperability, http://www.interop-vlab.eu) offered a workshop program comprising four workshops and a Doctorial Symposium. The objective of the workshops held on April 13th, 2010, was to strengthen some key topics related to interoperability for enterprise applications and software. The workshop organization left time slots for brainstorming among the attendees in order to come up with, at the end, possible new research directions. The Doctorial Symposium provides an open forum for students involved in the preparation of their PhDs to discuss their research issues and ideas with senior researchers.

It is a fact that enterprises need to collaborate if they want to survive in the current extreme dynamic and heterogenous business world they are involved in. Standards are a real key issue and an important activity to facilitate the interoperability of enterprise software. The goal of the workshop "*Standards – A Foundation for Interoperability*" is to increase awareness and understanding of interoperability standards as a fundamental need. SOA (Service Oriented Architecture) is now a widely used technology to implement industry-driven interoperability. The workshop "*Use of MDI/SOA Concepts in Industry*" promotes the application of MDI (Model Driven Interoperability) combined with SOA (Services Oriented Architecture) and the associated technology (BPM, Enterprise Modeling, ontology, mediation, model transformation, etc.) in industry. It presents the results from three projects: the "ISTA 3 project" (3rd generation interoperability for aeronautics suppliers), the "FP7 SHAPE project" (*Semantically-enabled heterogenous service architecture*) that extends SOA with semantics and heterogenous infrastructures and the "Interoperable Manufacturing Knowledge Systems" (IMKS) project. The workshop on "*Dynamic Management across Interoperating Enterprises*" investigates the need for enhancements to current business management systems and processes to address the needs of global trading across enterprises utilizing the new service-oriented Internet.

And finally, a *Doctoral Symposium* gave students involved in the preparation of their PhDs in any area of Interoperability for Enterprise Software and Applications the opportunity to present and discuss their research issues and ideas with senior researchers to better understand the interoperability context and issues.

We would like to express our thanks to the workshop chairs and committees for their contribution to the scientific success of these events.

Hervé Panetto, *CRAN UMR 7039, Nancy University, CNRS, France*
Herve.Panetto@cran.uhp-nancy.fr
Nacer Boudjlida, *LORIA UMR 7503, Nancy University, CNRS, France*
Nacer.Boudjlida@loria.fr

Standards
A Foundation for Interoperability

Standards – A Foundation for Interoperability

Martin Zelm, CIMOSA Association, Germany
David Chen, University of Bordeaux, France
martin.zelm@cimosa.de, david.chen@ims-bordeaux.fr

Standards Workshop Chairs' Message

The objective of this workshop was to increase awareness and understanding of interoperability standards. Standards play a fundamental role in achieving Enterprise Interoperability (EI) within and between enterprises. Interoperability works not only between information objects at the level of IT systems but also at the level of processes, resources, people and organizations. The six papers from standards initiatives identify issues related to enterprise interoperability. In the discussions, several proposals to improve the development and implementation of EI standards have been made, and will be followed via I-VLab and elsewhere:

– The standards development process of formal SDOs must receive full support from both national governments and from the European Union organizations to become more effective. Otherwise results obtained in R&D projects will be lost after completion of the project.

– Universities must strengthen their active involvement in the research and development of standards. A strong collaboration between research and standardization organizations is recommended, which should be supported by information dissemination and efforts to demonstrate results to increase public awareness and acceptance of both R&D and standardization results.

– The development of open, application-oriented EI standards in industry consortia (such as OMG or OASIS) is moving faster and with strong involvement from all stakeholders involved. However, governance of the implementation is limited to those involved, hence, such standards lack global acceptance.

– SME collaboration networks prefer sector-specific standards. This should be reflected in the classification of standards, as well as types of horizontal and vertical standards. The implementation of standards in SME networks is still in an early phase and often does not comply with the specifications.

Martin Zelm, *CIMOSA Association, Germany*
David Chen, *University of Bordeaux, France*

Standards for Enterprise Interoperation How to Improve?

Martin Zelm* — Kurt Kosanke**

c/o CIMOSA Association
* Hempenkamp 26
22359 Hamburg
Germany
martin.zelm@cimosa.de

**Stockholmer Str. 7
71034 Boeblingen
Germany
kosanke@cimosa.de

ABSTRACT. *Interoperation is the ability of two or more systems, applications or system components to exchange and use the exchanged information. This is especially important for enterprises engaged in collaboration and co-operation, which need a seamless exchange of products and services. Interoperation can be greatly enhanced through the use of global standards. The paper addresses standardization aspects in Enterprise Interoperation (EI). It presents an overview of EI standards and proposes a content-oriented category of such standards positioned in a layered hierarchy. Furthermore, the standards development process has been analyzed and proposals for improvement are made.*

KEYWORDS: *enterprise interoperation, categories of interoperability standards, standard development process*

1. Introduction

The increasing use of Information and Communication Technology (ICT) in business enterprises has caused a steep growth of business applications within those enterprises and across their industries. Due to the large variety of business applications, both vendors and users are urgently attempting to resolve this heterogenity in inter-organizational communication by interfacing and integrating the different applications [1].

Enterprises today face an even more challenging problem brought about by business globalization. This global environment has increased dramatically the need for intra-organizational communication, co-ordination, co-operation and collaboration. The corresponding need for interoperation of the related ICT-based business and technical processes has led to huge R&D efforts in both academia and industry, which in turn has initiated numerous standardization efforts in Standards Development Organizations (SDOs) and industry consortia. However, the large number of resulting standards often overlap or even contradict each other.

Companies that apply successful standards can gain significant competitive advantage. However, the choice of standards and their implementation have become a critical part of managing the IS function of an enterprise and developing its application software. At the same time, the scope, pace and success rate of standardization processes in SDOs have experienced problems [3]. Characterizing standards according to their application area will provide more clarity and better understanding of the role of standards in supporting enterprise interoperation on the different levels of the business.

2. General needs

The developers of technical standards for interoperation are generally concerned with interface standards, which detail how products or parts thereof interconnect with one another. In the vast field of standards, categories are important for an improved understanding of the context in which those standards are to be used.

One common category of interoperability standards makes a distinction between Core Standards and Content Standards [7]. Core standards define the basic concepts on a high level of abstraction to be employed in content standards. There is only a small quantity of such standards developed by worldwide SDOs as ISO/IEC, UN/CEFACT, W3C. There is consensus that core standards should remain stable or undergo only slight modifications. Content standards are to be employed by ICT users whether in an industry domain or in an application area. They can be directly deployed in software development and are intended to ensure the seamless exchange of information. There are many of these standards, often developed by user consortia and usually they are not really compliant with each other.

Another categorization could be made via a hierarchy of standards by organizing the standards according to their area of use. Such a hierarchy identifies levels for: i) standards for the development of standards, ii) standards for product development guidelines/constraints and iii) standards to be implemented in marketable products or services. This distinction separates the core standards mentioned above into two distinct levels, but defines content standards as standards to be implemented in products or product relevant standards.

Category	Purpose	Provider	User	Examples of standards for
Standards for standard developments	A general framework of concepts and guide lines used to develop standards	Researcher, SDOs and User Consortia together with Researcher	Software developer, system integrator	Enterprise reference architecture, (OMG-MDA, SOA), Application Integration,
Standards for product development	Information exchange between applications, within or across domains, Infrastructure services, multiple use	SDOs and User Consortia together with Software developer and system integrator	Industry consortia, Trade organizations, government agencies, product designer	Frameworks for Modeling, Interoperation, eBusiness, Modeling Languages, General ICT interfaces,
Standards for implementati on in products	Direct deployment in the design of product and services	Product /service application designer	Business end user	Product/service specific interfaces

Table 1. *Categories and properties of Enterprise Interoperability Standards*

The highest level of this hierarchy provides general standards, which identify basic concepts, their relationships and rules to guide their application in the standards development work. Examples are ISO/IEC 42010 *"Systems and Software Engineering — Architectural Description"* and ISO 15704 *"Reference-base for Enterprise Architectures and Models"* [5]. Such general frameworks are usually results of R&D work in both industry and academia and are brought into standardization by people involved in the R&D work. Such people have to stay involved in the full standardization process to achieve the successful completion of those standards.

The next lower level of the hierarchy identifies standards that define standardized means used to represent the content of implementable standards and guidelines for their development. However, such means usually cover a wide range of application areas and therefore these standards usually have multiple uses. Examples are standards for explicit usage for encoding data formats, like ISO/IEC 19776-1:2009: *"Extensible Mark-up Language"* *(XML)* or infrastructure standards like OMGs *"Web Services for Business Process Execution Language"* *(WS-BPEL)*, or standards still at framework level, but for a specific application domain, like

CEN/ISO 19439 "*Framework for Enterprise Modelling*", or ISO/CEN 11354-1 "*Framework for Enterprise Interoperability*". Some of these (like CEN/ISO 11354-1) can be seen as methods for assessing enterprise operations and thereby acting as precursors for both standard employment and developments. Again such standards are very much influenced by R&D work and the participation of the originators in the standards development process is crucial as well.

At the bottom level, we have product-relevant, implementable standards. Examples of such products that should be designed using standards for product development are enterprise modeling tools – plus the inherent language and methodology – that follow CEN/ISO 19439 "*Framework for Enterprise Modelling*" and also implement the language standard CEN/ISO 19440 "*Enterprise Integration - Constructs for Enterprise Modelling*", another of the intermediate level standards. At this level of the hierarchy, the participation of R&D personnel can also be productive. *A priori* knowledge of concepts, guidelines etc. will lead to high quality products that will find their place in the marketplace more easily.

Standards development is impacted by a number of issues such as for instance, the long development cycle times of 5 years or more. Due to changes in technology, the long standard development cycle creates a high risk for the end user. Hence, there is only very little involvement of users in the development of especially high level standards. Similarly the involvement of R&D personnel is rather limited in spite of being the originator of most of the high level standards and being potentially a valuable contributor to the lower level ones as well. The reason for the low involvement is a lack of funding for participation in standardization work. Such funding is available at best only during R&D projects and is therefore not aligned with the time schedule of standardization work. Standardization work can only start with some early results of the project, but usually ends much later than the R&D work.

3. Standards for Enterprise Interoperation

We intend to follow the above three-layer hierarchy and consider the categories of standards to develop standards, standards for product developments, and implementable standards, all from the viewpoint of Enterprise Interoperation.

A categorization of standards related to Enterprise Interoperation has been proposed by Kosanke [4]. Figure 1 presents an overview of standards related to interoperation for use both by standard developers and standard users. The category General Standards can be considered as standards for standards at the high level, whereas the categories of Frameworks, Languages and Related Standards are standards at the medium level.

The intention of these standards is to describe the enterprise in models and use of those models to identify and resolve interoperability problems. ISO 14258

"*Concepts and Rules for Enterprise Models*", identifies requirements for standards on model interoperability and defines three ways in which models can interoperate with each other:

– integrated (use of common modeling form);

– unified (use of common meta-level structure);

– federated (use of model characterization to dynamically accommodate different models).

General Standards		
ISO/IEC 42010 *"Systems and software engineering — Architectural description"*		
ISO 14258 *"Concepts and rules for enterprise models"*		
ISO 15704 *"Reference-base for enterprise architectures and models"* (Needs for Frameworks, Methodologies, Languages, Tools, Models, Modules)		
ISO 27387 *"Reference for process modelling methods"*		
OMG BPMN *"Business Process Modelling Notation"*		
Frameworks	Languages	Related Standards
CEN/ISO 19439 *"Framework for modelling"*	**CEN/ISO 19440** *"Constructs for modelling*	**ENV 13550** **"Model execution** *services"* (EMEIS)
ISO 15745 *"Framework for application integration*	**ISO 18629** *"Process specification language"*	**ISO 15531** *"Mfg. mgmt. data exchange"*
ISO 15288 *"Life cycle management"*	**ISO/IEC 15414** *"ODP enterprise language"*	**ISO 16100** *"Mfg. software capability profiling*
CEN/ISO 11354 *"Enterprise process interoperability"*	**OMG BPEL4WS** *"Business Process Execution Language"*	**ISO 18435** **"Diagnostics, capability** *assessment, and maintenance applications integration"*
ISO/IEC 10746 (ODP) **"Open distributed** *processing"*	**OASIS ebXML** **"e-Business using** *eXtensible Mark-up Language"*	
OMG MDA **"Model Driven** *Architecture"*		**IEC/ISO 62264** *"Control systems integration"*
	OMG UML *"Unified Modelling Language"*	**OMG BPDM** **"Business Process** *Definition Metamodel"*

Figure 1. *Overview of standards related to Enterprise Interoperation [4]*

However, integration and unification are special cases, which can only be achieved in their true meaning for a limited time period, due to the need for evolution – a property of any system in use. Therefore, the most important scenario for interoperation of enterprise models, processes and applications is the federated situation. Information about capabilities and needs of the entities participating in an interoperation could support such federated interoperations. Such information concerning e.g. information syntax and semantic could be provided *a priori* by profiles identifying those needs and capabilities.

A severe problem is impacting the deployment of standards for interoperation. Such standards are almost unknown in industry and the promotion of interoperability standards and their specific benefits is very weak. The standards are often only known to a small group of experts involved in their development. The promotion of interoperation standards and their specific benefits to a large public audience is urgently needed. This could occur in publications, presentations at workshops and conferences and demonstrations of pilot implementations.

However, to really increase the visibility of interoperability standards in the industry, new sources of funding or new business models must be established to obtain the required visibility.

A very special audience is the SME community, which has a similar problem in attending promotion events as for the participation in standard developments: availability of competent personnel. This audience could most easily be reached through their national and regional professional and business associations.

4. The standards development process: concerns

ISO standards for ICT are developed within working groups, decisions are consensus-based, participation is voluntary and industry wide open [5]. Standard users have to buy the standard, since they intend to benefit from its content. The public at large, however, does not have any access to standards documentation – except by paying a rather high fee. This creates severe problems for information dissemination, changes for further R&D developments and even a potential increase of interoperability standards deployment.

In a White Paper *"Modernising ICT Standardisation in the EU – The Way Forward"*, the European Commission [2] defines various requirements on standards and standardization policies and emphasizes their importance in the global economy. However, very little – over and above suggesting the establishment of a permanent, multi-stakeholder ICT standardization policy platform – is said on how such standards can be developed and about the necessary financial support. This matches the observation that explicit standardization projects are usually not funded.

The most important needs to strengthen the impact of ICT standards on interoperability are: i) a faster, more efficient development process; this could mean adopting and enhancing the ISO Fast Track Process [6], or learning from the experience of industry consortia; ii) a business model for public funding of standards development process; researchers cannot do the standardization work without financial support; iii) the need for strong promotion of standards. The users community has to be convinced of the business value of standardized interoperation and the SDOs should understand that providing relevant documentation to research organizations free of charge can increase their sales potential.

5. Concluding remarks

Looking at standards for interoperation we have investigated two issues: first, how to improve the understanding of such standards and their relationships by positioning them in a three-layer structure; second, identifying deficiencies and needs in the current standards development process.

Both an improved standardization process and a better understanding on scope and intended audience of relevant standardization carry a high potential to increase quality, understanding, timely availability and employment of interoperability standards and make enterprise interoperation more efficient. Better and more efficient information dissemination, as well as availability of documentation, will support these efforts and especially the latter will offer more goal-orientated R&D work.

Only if new methods of public funding – not only for R&D work but for the related standards development as well – come into place will the currently unsatisfactory situation in employment of interoperability standards improve.

6. References

[1] Chen D., Doumeingts G., "European initiatives to develop interoperability of enterprise applications – basic concepts, framework and roadmap", *Annual Reviews in Control 27*, 2003, p. 153–162

[2] European Commission, "Modernising ICT Standardisation in the EU – The Way Forward", COM 324, 2009

[3] King J., Lyytinen K. (Eds), "Standards making: A critical research frontier for information systems", *MSI Quarterly Special Issue*, 2003

[4] Kosanke K., Martin R., "Enterprise and Business Processes – How to Interoperate? The Standards View", *Workshop on Standards for Interoperability*, held at I-ESA'08, www.interop-vlab.eu/, 2008.

[5] ISO-2, "How are ISO Standards Developed?" www.iso.rg, 2010

[6] ISO-1, "ISO Fast Track Process", www.iso.org, 2009

[7] Rowell, M., "Oracle, OAGIS and Open Standards", 2008, http://www.oagi.org/

Framework for Enterprise Interoperability and Maturity Model (CEN/ISO 11354)

David Chen*[1]

IMS – University of Bordeaux
351, cours de la libération
33405 Talence
France
david.chen@ims-bordeaux.fr

ABSTRACT. *This paper presents an on-going international standardization initiative jointly carried out by CEN TC310/WG1 and ISO TC184 SC5/WG1 to define and standardize a Framework for Enterprise Interoperability (FEI) and a Maturity Model for Enterprise Interoperability (MMEI). The standard aims at providing a common understanding of the enterprise interoperability domain and defining metrics for measuring interoperability maturity levels of an enterprise.*

KEYWORDS: *Interoperability, Framework, Maturity Model, Standard, Enterprise system*

1 The author thanks David Shorter and Kurt Kosanke (both are member of CEN/TC310/WG1 and ISO/TC184/SC5/WG1) for their contributions to this standardization work.

1. Introduction

Standards play an important role to achieve interoperability. Besides various standards developed in specific technological domains, this paper focuses on conceptual standards which are independent from particular technologies. Those standards are important to achieve a common understanding on interoperability problems, domain and metric. The standard CEN/ISO 11354, jointly developed by CEN/TC310/WG1 and ISO TC184 SC5/WG1, aims at elaborating a Framework for Enterprise Interoperability which defines the enterprise interoperability domain in terms of its problem and solution spaces, and proposing a maturity model for evaluating interoperability levels. The standard is based on the research initially performed at IMS/University of Bordeaux under the umbrella of several European projects relating to interoperability: IDEAS (2002), ATHENA (2003) and INTEROP (2003).

Interoperability is the ability to communicate and exchange information and use the exchanged information (IEEE, 1990), and to access functionality of a third system. Enterprise Interoperability is considered to be significant, if it can take place at least, at three levels (data, process and business) with a semantic defined in the related context (IDEAS, 2002). This standard is based on the assumptions that: (i) enterprise systems are not interoperable because of barriers to interoperability; (ii) barriers are incompatibilities of various kinds at the various enterprise levels; (iii) there are common barriers to interoperability and generic solutions to remove barriers.

The paper is structured as follow: section 2 identifies/defines basic concepts of enterprise interoperability and presents a Framework for Enterprise Interoperability (FEI). In section 3 the Maturity Model for Enterprise Interoperability (MMEI) is outlined. A Kiviat graph is used to represent the result of an interoperability assessment. Section 4 discusses related work. Finally, section 5 concludes the paper.

2. Framework for Enterprise Interoperability (FEI)

The Framework for Enterprise Interoperability aims at structuring basic enterprise interoperability concepts and issues. The framework has three basic dimensions: (i) *interoperability concerns* that define the content of interoperation that may take place at various levels of the enterprise (data, service, process, business); (ii) *interoperability barriers* that identify various obstacles to interoperability in three categories (conceptual, technological, organisational); (iii) *interoperability approaches* that represent the different ways in which barriers can be removed (integrated, unified and federated).

The first two dimensions: interoperability concerns and interoperability barriers constitute the problem space of enterprise interoperability. The intersection of an interoperability barrier and an interoperability concern is the set of interoperability problems having the same barrier and concern. The three dimensions of the framework (see Figure 1) constitute the solution space of enterprise interoperability. The intersection of an interoperability barrier, an interoperability concern and an interoperability approach is the set of solutions to the breakdown of that interoperability barrier existing for the particular concern and using the selected approach.

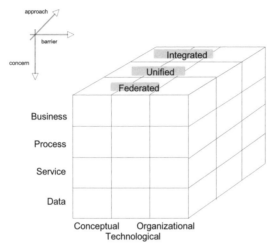

Figure 1. *Enterprise interoperability framework*

The FEI defines the domain of enterprise interoperability. It allows us to capture and structure interoperability knowledge and solutions according to their ability to remove interoperability barriers. For example, PSL (Process Specification Language) is a standard solution (ISO 18629) that contributes to the removal of *conceptual* barriers (both syntax and semantics) concerning *process* interoperability using a *unified* approach.

3. Maturity Model for Enterprise Interoperability (MMEI)

The maturity model will enable an assessment of an enterprise's ability to interoperate with another enterprise. MMEI is built on the FEI described above and covers the whole problem space of the FEI (four interoperability concerns and three kinds of interoperability barrier). Five levels of interoperability maturity are defined as shown in Table 1. Each level identifies a certain degree of ability to interoperate with another enterprise.

Maturity Level	Maturity assessment
Level 4 - Adaptive	Capable of negotiating and dynamically accommodating with any heterogenous partner
Level 3 - Organized	Capable of meta modeling for mapping in order to interoperate with multiple heterogenous partners
Level 2 - Aligned	Capable of making necessary changes to align to common formats or standards
Level 1 - Defined	Capability of properly modeling and describing systems to prepare interoperability
Level 0 - Unprepared	Not relevant: there is no ability for interoperation

Table 1. *Interoperability maturity levels*

Levels 0 and 1 correspond to the situation where there are no or only a few abilities for ad hoc interoperations. From levels 2 to 4, three levels of maturity are defined that correspond to the three Interoperability Approach dimensions of the FEI (Integrated, Unified and Federated). Table 2 shows the mapping between maturity levels and interoperation environments.

Maturity Level	Interoperation environments
Level 4 - Adaptive	Federated: no pre-defined format or meta-models. Dynamically adjust and accommodate
Level 3 - Organized	Unified: use of meta-models allowing heterogenous systems to map one to others
Level 2 - Aligned	Integrated: common format (or standard) for all partners to build their systems (components)
Level 1 - Defined	Connected: simple electronic exchange of information, messaging, etc.
Level 0 - Unprepared	Isolated: occasional and manual exchange of information (document, fax, etc.)

Table 2. *Maturity levels vs. interoperation environments*

Each level of maturity also corresponds to a degree of interoperability ranging from no interoperability to full interoperability as shown in Table 3.

Maturity Level	Interoperability degree
Level 4 - Adaptive	Generalized (full interoperability to any potential partner)
Level 3 - Organized	Extended (many-to-many multiple heterogenous partners)
Level 2 - Aligned	Restricted (Peer-to-peer, to use common format/standard)
Level 1 - Defined	Limited (with only some ad hoc interoperations)
Level 0 - Unprepared	Nonexistent

Table 3. *Maturity levels and interoperability degree*

Table 4 gives a high level view of MMEI and shows the main focus for each combination of each maturity level and for each interoperability barrier category.

Maturity Levels/ Barriers	Conceptual	Technological	Organizational
Level 4 - Adaptive	Accommodated	Reconfigurable	Agile
Level 3 - Organized	Mapped	Open-architecture	Trained
Level 2 - Aligned	Adhered	Arranged	Flexible
Level 1 - Defined	Modeled	Connectable	Specified
Level 0 - Unprepared	Incomplete	Inaccessible	Inexplicit

Table 4. *Focus of concerns in MMEI*

Each maturity level is described in detail with a table based on the FEI (dimensions of interoperability concerns and interoperability barriers). Each cell defines requirements (or criteria to meet) which are necessary to reach that interoperability maturity level. The transition from one level to a higher one corresponds generally to a removal of interoperability barriers and satisfaction of requirements. An example of these tables is shown in Table 5, which shows the details of level 0.

		Conceptual	Technological	Organizational
Level 0	Business	Visions, strategies, politics not properly described	No IT infrastructure /platform in place	Undefined organization structure
	Process	Processes not formally described	Manual processes	Undefined /undocumented methods of work
	Service	Services not formally defined	Stand-alone services	Responsibilities /authorities for services not known
	Data	Heterogenous data representation, not completely modeled	Closed data storage devices, manual exchange	Responsibilities /authorities for data not defined

Table 5. *Description of the maturity level 0*

The initial level of interoperability maturity is characterized by proprietary (heterogenous) nature of systems. All the systems resources are not meant to be shared with other systems. Systems modeling and description are not complete or even not existent. The organization is not explicitly specified. There is in general no capability for interoperation with other companies. Communication remains on the level of manual exchange. Systems run stand-alone and are not prepared for interoperability (Guédria *et al.*, 2009).

The interoperability assessment results of an enterprise can be represented in different ways. Figure 2[2] shows one such representation as a Kiviat graph (radar plot) that allows us to represent the 5 maturity levels in relation to the 4 concerns

---

2 Originally proposed by K. Kosanke and D. Shorter.

and 3 barrier types identified in the FEI. Figure 2 also shows an illustrative example of an assessment of two enterprises' interoperability capabilities (blue and red lines). Depending on the enterprise goal to reach a particular capability level being 1, 2, 3 or 4, the sufficient and missing capabilities can be identified. In the example, for the blue enterprise the organizational capabilities of the business maturity level do not even reach level 1 whereas the conceptual and technological capabilities reach up to maturity level 3 for process and service and data, respectively. If level 2 were the desired one for the intended cooperation between two enterprises, improvements would have to be made in technological capabilities on the business concern and in organizational capabilities on the three concerns: business, process and data.

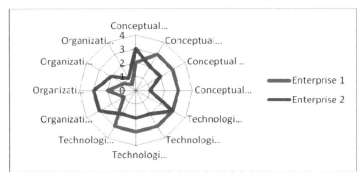

Figure 2. *Interoperability maturity assessment (kinds of barrier and concern)*

4. Related works

The FEI is based on existing interoperability frameworks (i.e. IDEAS Interoperability framework (IDEAS, 2003), ATHENA interoperability framework (ATHENA, 2003), European Interoperability Framework (EIF, 2004) etc.). These frameworks do not address barriers to interoperability explicitly; they are not aimed at structuring interoperability knowledge according to the ability to remove various barriers and solve problems. Mapping between the FEI and existing frameworks are provided in the annex of the standard on that this paper is based. MMEI is based on the FEI but influenced by existing approaches: LISI (Levels of Information Systems Interoperability) (C4ISR, 1998), OIM (Organizational Interoperability Model) (Clark *et al.*, 1999), LCIM (Levels of Conceptual Interoperability Model) (Tolk *et al.*, 2003), EIMM (Enterprise Interoperability Maturity Model) (Athena, 2003) and ISO/15504 (SPICE). The latter is not dedicated to interoperability issues. Existing maturity models focus, in most cases, on one simple facet of interoperability (data, technology, conceptual, enterprise modeling, etc.). They are complementary rather than contradictory. Consequently MMEI aims at structuring the different approaches into a single complete interoperability maturity model to avoid redundancy and ensure consistency.

5. Conclusions

With respect to existing frameworks (ATHENA, IDEAS, EIF, etc.), FEI is barrier-driven. If a problem or a solution cannot find its place in the framework, it is not related to an interoperability concern per se. Incompatibility is the fundamental concept used in defining the FEI. It is the obstacle to establishing seamless interoperation. The concept of "incompatibility" has a broad sense and is not only limited to the "technical" aspect usually considered in the IT domain, but also includes "information" and "organization", and concerns all levels of the enterprise.

MMEI is defined on the basis of the FEI and is consistent with it. It is to note that a lower interoperability maturity for a company does not mean a systematic dysfunction at all levels and for all functions of the company. The maturity is only evaluated from the interoperability point of view and cannot be applied for other purposes. A high level degree of interoperability cannot be achieved for free. It is generally costly and time consuming. Each enterprise must define its interoperability requirements and maturity level to be reached. It is not recommended to look for the highest interoperability level regardless of their needs.

6. References

ATHENA, (2003) *Advanced Technologies for Interoperability of Heterogenous Enterprise Networks and their Applications*, FP6-2002-IST-1, Integrated Project.

C4ISR (1998) Architecture Working Group (AWG), Levels of Information Systems Interoperability (LISI).

Clark T., Jones R. (1999), "Organisational interoperability maturity model for c2", in *Proc. of the Command and Control Research and Technology Symposium*, Washington.

EIF, CompTIA: European Industry Association. "European Interoperability Framework" White Paper - ICT Industry Recommendations, http://www.comptia.org, (2004).

Guédria W., Chen D. and Naudet Y., *A Maturity Model for Enterprise Interoperability*, IFAC/IFIP workshop (EI2N2009), Vilamoura (Portugal), November 3-4, 2009.

IDEAS (2002) Consortium, Thematic Network, IDEAS: Interoperability Development for Enterprise Application and Software – Roadmaps, Annex1 – Description of Work.

IEEE, (1990) IEEE Standard Computer Dictionary: A Compilation of IEEE Standard Computer Glossaries.

INTEROP, (2003) Interoperability Research for Networked Enterprises Applications and Software, Network of Excellence, Proposal Part B.

ISO/IEC 15504, Software Process Improvement and Capability DEtermination Model (SPICE) (2001).

Tolk A., Muguira J.A. (2003), "The levels of conceptual interoperability model", in *2003 Fall Simulation Interoperability Workshop*, USA.

Testing Interoperability Standards – A Test Case Generation Methodology

Nenad Ivezic* — Jungyub Woo*

* 100 Bureau Drive
Gaithersburg, MD 20899
United States
nenad.ivezic@nist.gov
jungyub.woo@nist.gov

ABSTRACT. *Over many years, the National Institute of Standards and Technology (NIST) has built test beds to support interoperability standards development and their implementation within software applications. A general test framework has been proposed to enhance new test bed development and reuse of existing test components and materials. Currently, the test framework is undergoing a validation effort within a healthcare domain to develop a test case generation facility.*

KEYWORDS: *interoperability, standards, testing, test bed, test framework, NIST*

1. Introduction

The National Institute of Standards and Technology (NIST) has built numerous test beds to support interoperability standards development and their implementation within software applications for industries such as automotive, construction and healthcare.

Currently, individual test beds are being built almost from scratch with very limited reuse of existing test materials and components. This is not cost effective and is problematic from the perspective of advancing knowledge of testing. Existing testing approaches and frameworks do not address the issue of reuse to any significant extent (IIC, 2010; RosettaNet 2004; TTCN-3, 2010; TaMIE, 2010).

For that reason, NIST started to develop a general test framework to provide a vehicle for generalization and accumulation of knowledge of testing while providing a platform for management and reuse of test materials and test components.

Presently, we are validating the test framework on a number of industrial test cases. In this paper, we describe an application of the test framework to establish a unified test case generation methodology and to design an architectural solution for a supporting test case generation tool.

2. A general test framework: test case design

A key consideration when developing a test framework is that it should support a variety of alternative testing modes including independent document validation, individual application conformance, and peer-to-peer (or interoperability) testing. Also, the test framework should allow easy adaptation of test materials to any of the above testing scenarios.

The NIST-proposed test framework allows capture of test materials from the underlying domain and business perspectives and without reference to a specific testing configuration or role that test components and system under test (SUT) may assume (Ivezic *et al.*, 2010). This is in contrast to most existing test case designs that depend on both a standard specification and a specific test bed implementation or testing configuration.

Additionally, to allow easy adaptation of the test materials, the test framework includes a test case architecture containing two layers: an abstract test case and executable test case. An abstract test case is derived, in general, from standard specifications and the intended usage patterns for the system under test. Its purpose is to specify the validation rules and testing procedure at an abstract level. Validation rules are written using logical conditions; that is, they describe the normative requirements based on the standard specifications. The testing procedure describes the usage patterns that are simulated for the system under test (SUT).

Abstract test cases are intended for human consumption and may be thought of as a meta-model for the executable test cases. This implies that the abstract test case is independent of a specific test bed implementation and testing configuration. On the other hand, an executable test case is an implementation of the abstract test case that executes the validation process. Consequently, the executable test case contains machine-readable content that reflects a specific test bed and test configuration.

Another key issue for existing test frameworks is that a typical test case design embeds verification rules as an integral part of the testing procedure. These verification rules are used to ascertain whether the test items are true with respect to the test requirements. In this way, these two parts of the test case are closely coupled, because the verification rules will be executed at a specific point in time within the testing procedure. This approach, however, gives rise to two types of problems. First, test cases tend to be monolithic, large, and difficult to maintain. Also, test case design is difficult to modify when the underlying standards change. The second problem is low reusability. Since verification rules are based on the SUT test requirements and testing is based on the business scenarios in which the SUT participates, numerous combinations are possible. The tight coupling means that each such combination will require significant changes to the test cases.

To overcome these problems the NIST-proposed test framework contains a modular design for test cases, in which the test cases consist of procedural content and verification rules. Each test case (either the abstract or executable test case) is composed of two scripts. One script contains procedural content: a usage script for the abstract test case and a procedure script for the executable test case. The other script contains verification content: an assertion for the abstract test case and a verification script for the executable test case.

The two procedural scripts are distinguished by their intent and time of specification. The usage script in the abstract test case represents the testing-related business process, which includes the partners' life cycles and actions during testing. Actions are abstract descriptions and contain no message instances. For example, the usage script may say "Buyer sends a purchase order message to a Supplier." The specific buyer, purchase order, and supplier instances are not yet specified. On the other hand, the procedural script in the executable test case represents a business transaction that will be executed and contains specific instances and references to actors in the business process.

Verification scripts contain event-driven conditions, which must be satisfied before the verification script is activated (triggered). When the activation condition is satisfied, a test item, such as a document or a message, is verified against an assertion. These activation conditions render the verification rule independent of the testing procedure, since the rule is not activated at a specific step of testing procedure. Consequently, verification scripts may be reused readily within a new testing procedure because the verification script is independently executed by the events during the test procedure.

Verification scripts are distinguished by their intent and time of specification. The assertion script in the abstract test case is human-, not machine-, readable because a specific verifier may be unknown at development time. When that verifier is known, the Test Case Developer can add assertion codes using an executable language. This assertion code is the verification script in the executable test case.

3. A test framework validation: test case generation tooling

Test generation, within any realistically complex domain, is a complex task that involves management of evolving testing requirements, capturing correct intent of these requirements, and efficient management of change in any aspect of the testing process. Within the healthcare domain, NIST is developing a test case generation methodology that can span numerous healthcare sub-domains and interoperability profiles. The NIST framework is used to architect the test case generation tooling.

The essential goal for a test case generation tool is to facilitate specification, generation, and traceability of test cases. Specification entails representation of testing requirements in an abstract form that enables computational assessment whether a system under test has met the requirements. Generation entails transformation of an abstract test form into an executable form that may be run on a specific computational platform. Traceability entails capturing relationships among requirements, decisions made in the testing execution environment, the resulting abstract test forms, and executable forms of test cases. Additional usability and operational requirements for the facility include maintenance of complete specifications in a so called intermediate form. This form maintains complete information required to create executable test cases.

Figure 1 illustrates the workflow that the facility will support and its three operational stages. At Stage 1, the facility enables interactions with users in support of test case specification. Here, test case requirements are captured through interaction with the Test User to obtain test case setup information and with the Test Case Developer to identify key Test Events from the underlying Test Requirements materials. As a result of this stage, the Abstract Test Case Repository is populated for the testing objectives at hand. In addition to the previously introduced Usage Script and Assertion Script test artefacts, the Message Template artefact is introduced with the role to provide schema-type constraint information for the test messages to be created. Since the Abstract Test Case does not consider test specifics, the message template has no specific values assigned and will be used to generate a message instance or validation context file at Stage 2.

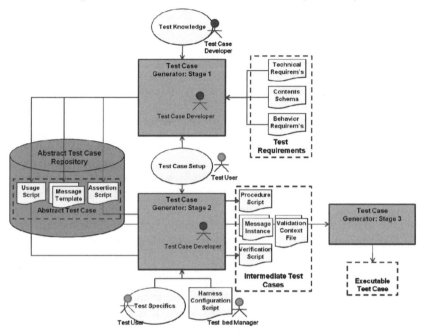

Figure 1. *Test case generator facility and its operational stages*

At Stage 2, the facility enables interactions with users in support of additional specification of the test execution environment. The run-time information is captured through interaction with the Test User's additional setup information as well as the test specifics, e.g. test model or test message data definition. The test harness configuration and role assignments of the test modules, such as validation service or message handling, and SUT(s) are specified through interaction with the Test Bed Manager. The procedure scripts identify required message instances that will be sent during testing. Additionally, the facility provides a graphical user interface for Test Users to generate message instances from the message templates. To validate a message from a SUT, Test Case Developer uses the message template to create a validation context file with expected values for the test object sent by the SUT. The outcome of this stage is the Intermediate Test Case collection with sufficient information about test cases and execution environment to support automated generation of executable test cases at Stage 3.

To be successful, the framework and the test generation facility will have to be supportive of a wide range of testing use cases across the different industries. An iterative prototype-evaluate-refine approach to the validation of test generation facility is adopted with an initial focus on the healthcare industry.

4. Impacting testing interoperability standards

When testing interoperability standards, an organization utilizes different modes of testing including independent document validation, individual application conformance, and peer-to-peer/interoperability testing. The exact testing strategy for interoperability standards will depend on many factors such as the complexity of applications, size of the community, the time horizon for implementing and management of the standards, and so on.

Traditionally, the underlying test materials were captured within procedural statements tied to a specific testing mode as well as a specific testing configuration. This approach has proven to be unwieldy and hard to manage because the logical definitions of correctness of an implementation are buried within the testing procedures that deal with run-time testing issues such as test bed configuration and test material execution.

With the proposed test framework facility and the test case design in place, the logic of testing is not encumbered by the specific testing mode, configuration and execution concerns any longer. As a consequence, it is much easier to move from one mode of testing to another, from one test bed configuration to another (e.g. from a single simulation node to multi-simulation node test bed), and from one type of execution environment to another (e.g. from one configuration of Web services to another).

From the perspective of advancing the knowledge of testing interoperability standards, the proposed testing framework and test case design are initial steps in the direction of abstracting and organizing the testing knowledge for greater efficiency and transparency. Without a concentrated effort to agree on conceptualizations in the testing space, the ability to share and reuse test components and test beds for interoperability standards testing will continue to be very limited.

5. Conclusion

Presently, test case designs give rise to closely coupled, monolithic and difficult-to-maintain test cases. Since test cases are difficult to modify when the underlying standards change, low reusability of test materials follows. To overcome these problems, the proposed test framework contains a modular test case design where the test cases consist of procedural content and verification rules. Also, the framework introduces the notion of abstract test case, which is independent of a specific test bed implementation. In the first validation of the test framework, the test framework methodology is assessed in the context of health care scenarios and the requirements to support specification, generation, and traceability of test cases.

6. Acknowledgements

Certain commercial software products identified in this paper were used only for demonstration purposes. This use does not imply approval or endorsement by NIST, nor does it imply these products are necessarily the best available for the purpose.

7. References

IIC ("ebXML IIC Test Framework Version 1.0." OASIS), on-line at http://www.oasis-open.org/committees/download.php/1990/ebXML-TestFramework-10.zip, accessed March 2010.

Ivezic, N., Woo, J., Cho, H., "Towards Test Framework for Efficient and Reusable Global e-Business Test Beds", in *Proceedings of I-ESA 2010 Conference*, Coventry, UK, 2010.

RosettaNet (RosettaNet Ready Self-Test Kit (STK) User's Guide Release Version 2.0.7). RosettaNet, 2004.

TaMIE Site, on-line at http://www.oasis-open.org/committees/tamie, accessed March 2010.

TTCN-3 site, on-line at http://www.ttcn-3.org, accessed March 2010.

OMG Specifications for Enterprise Interoperability

Brian Elvesæter* — Arne-Jørgen Berre*

* SINTEF ICT
P. O. Box 124 Blindern
N-0314 Oslo
Norway
brian.elvesater@sintef.no
arne.j.berre@sintef.no

ABSTRACT. Enterprise Interoperability is a term that describes a field of activity with the aim to improve the manner in which enterprises, by means of information and communications technology (ICT), interoperate with other enterprises, organizations. To meet these challenges, enterprises are today looking into enterprise architectures. The Object Management Group (OMG) is an international, open membership and not-for-profit industry consortium, which develops enterprise integration standards for a wide range of technologies and provides modeling standards to support enterprise architecture. In this paper we give an overview of the newest OMG modeling standard initiatives with respect to enterprise architecture.

KEYWORDS: model-driven architecture, enterprise interoperability, enterprise architecture

1. Introduction

Enterprise Interoperability [Li, *et al.* 2006] is a term that describes a field of activity with the aim of improving the manner in which enterprises, by means of information and communications technology (ICT), interoperate with other enterprises, organizations, or with other business units of the same enterprise, in order to conduct their business. To meet these challenges, enterprises are today looking into enterprise architectures that provide models that can be used to describe and understand how different aspects of an enterprise work together. A framework for enterprise architecture was first introduced by Zachman in 1987 [Zachman 1987] and today there are several, such as DoDAF [Department of Defense] and MODAF [Ministry of Defence], and TOGAF [The Open Group] that allows you to define your own custom framework.

Regardless of the differences between the enterprise architectures, the models within them must all represent the goals, processes, rules, IT resources and relationships that define how the enterprise operates. The Object Management Group (OMG) is an international, open membership and not-for-profit industry consortium, which develops enterprise integration standards for a wide range of technologies and provides modeling standards to support enterprise architecture. Since all of OMG's modeling specifications are based on a common modeling infrastructure, namely the Meta-Object Facility (MOF) [OMG 2006], using OMG modeling standards helps tie individual models together in an overall architecture.

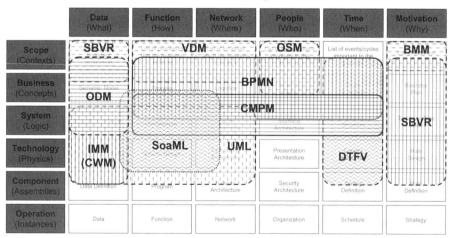

Figure 1. *Positioning the OMG specifications in the Zachman Framework*

In this paper we give an overview of the newest OMG modeling standard initiatives with respect to enterprise architecture. Figure 1 shows the Zachman Framework populated with the OMG specifications discussed in this paper. Section

2 of the paper describes the standards for business modeling, while section 3 describes the standards for IT modeling. Finally, section 4 concludes the paper.

2. OMG standards for business modeling

The OMG Business Ecology Initiative [BEI] is an industry collaboration forum that brings together best practices in process management with the aim of providing standards, relationship and communication mechanisms for IT and business alignment. OMG has several standards underway. Below we give a short presentation of some of the new modeling standard initiatives with respect to business modeling.

2.1. Business Motivation Model (BMM)

Implementing enterprise architecture typically starts with documenting goals, strategy and business plans. The Business Motivation Model (BMM) specification [OMG 2008a] provides a scheme or structure for developing, communicating and managing business plans in an organized manner. BMM defines a set of concepts (e.g. goal, objective, vision, means and strategy) that can be used to model the elements of business plans. These elements can be linked to business roles, business rules and organization unit that are specified using other OMG modeling standards.

2.2. Business Process Modeling Notation (BPMN)

The Business Process Modeling Notation (BPMN), Version 2.0 [OMG 2009a] is in the final stages of standards adoption at OMG. The specification provides a notation and a model for business processes and an interchange format that can be used to exchange BPMN process definitions between different tools.

BPMN is designed to cover many types of modeling and allows the creation of end-to-end business processes. It allows the specification of private processes (both non-executable and executable), public processes, choreographies and collaborations. Private processes are those internal to a specific organization. A public process represents the interactions between a private business process and another process or participant. While a standard business process describes the flow of activities within a specific business entity or organization, a choreography formalizing the way business participants coordinate their interactions. The focus of a choreography is on the exchange of messages between the participants. A collaboration depicts the interaction between two or more business entities.

BPMN is constrained to support only the concepts of modeling that are applicable to business processes. Other types of modeling, e.g. organizational models, data models, strategy models and business rules models are formalized in other OMG specifications.

2.3. *Organization Structure Metamodel (OSM)*

A request for proposal (RFP) for an Organization Structure Metamodel (OSM) was issued back in 2004 [OMG 2004]. The objective was to define a metamodel to be used for specification of organization structure. An organization structure metamodel consists of modeling elements used to represent organizational entities, their organizational sub-units and organizational attributes, and relationships of the organization units and people assigned to them. There has been some initial work on this specification, but it has been delayed due to limited resources and the demands for other specifications. A re-issue of the RFP is currently being discussed within the OMG.

2.4. *Value Delivery Metamodel (VDM)*

A Value Delivery Metamodel (VDM) RFP [OMG 2009b] has recently been issued. This RFP solicits proposals for a metamodel specification for modeling customer value delivery. Integrated value delivery models provide context for understanding the impact of services on multiple lines of business, and helps configuring new lines of business, making use of existing or new business services. These models also provide the context for sharing services. They make cost and time analysis, in the context of strategic planning and transformation, more efficient by formalizing the structure of the value delivery system. They provide linkage of improvement initiatives to the value proposition, and through this provide visibility in performance gaps and set priorities for process improvement. They serve as the ideal vehicle for alignment for business and IT, and are particularly suited for analysis in networked enterprise context. These models can additionally serve as basis for monitoring business and business performance in these networks.

2.5. *Case Management Process Modeling (CMPM)*

A Case Management Process Modeling (CMPM) RFP [OMG 2009c] has recently been issued. This RFP solicits proposals for a metamodel extension to BPMN 2.0 to support modeling of case management processes. Case Management focuses on actions to resolve a case – a situation to be managed toward objectives. Cases don't have predefined processes for achieving objectives. Humans make decisions based on observations, experience and the case file. Changes in the state of the case will result in new actions. A practice/discipline may adopt rules to guide decisions and make processes more repeatable. New modeling paradigms are required to facilitate all this. Case management is typically suited to manage knowledge work, and in particular work that is associated with innovation activities and initiatives.

2.6. *Semantics of Business Vocabulary and Business Rules (SBVR)*

The Semantics of Business Vocabulary and Business Rules (SBVR) specification [OMG 2008b] provides the means to precisely define business vocabularies so that they are interpretable in formal logic. A business vocabulary is a special purpose language, a body of terms each with a particular technical meaning, as used in different business domains. Business vocabularies are concept centric. The SBVR specification provides a hierarchical categorization of vocabularies, allowing concepts to be organized from the general to the specific, and also handles synonyms, abbreviations, cross-references and multiple vocabularies.

SBVR also support the definition of governance rules that use the terms in the business vocabularies. SBVR rules are expressed in natural language to allow them to be easily read and written by business practitioners.

2.7. *Date-Time Foundation Vocabulary (DTFV)*

Many business rules involve common, generic, cross-domain concepts such as date and time. Vendors and users of tools that capture and implement business rules need standard vocabularies for such concepts to improve interoperability among tools. OMG wants to promote the SBVR standard and issued the Date-Time Foundation Vocabulary (DTFV) RFP in 2008 that requests an SBVR vocabulary for date and time. The RFP additionally requests date-time vocabulary to be delivered as an ODM ontology and a UML model, so that the shared set of concepts can be linked by cross-references among the models.

3. OMG standards for IT modeling

The OMG Model Driven Architecture [MDA] defines a model-driven approach to software development where models are positioned as a first-class artefact. MDA promotes portability of software applications by allowing the same models to be realized on multiple underlying technology platforms such as CORBA, Java Enterprise Edition (JEE), .NET and Web Services through model mappings and transformation. MDA also aims to improve integration and interoperability based on models of different domain applications and component interfaces. Below we give a short presentation of some of the new modeling standard initiatives with respect to IT modeling.

3.1. *Unified Modeling Language (UML)*

The Unified Modeling Language (UML) [OMG 2009d, OMG 2009e] is probably OMG's best known specification. The language itself is a collection of 13 different graphical modeling notations that were designed to show different aspects of software design during the development process. It is widely supported by different tool vendors. UML defines an extension mechanism that allows the specification of specialized UML-based languages, so-called UML profiles, to be easily created and supported in modeling tools.

UML has been criticized for being positioned as the one-size fits all when it comes to IT modeling languages. As can be seen from Figure 1, this is definitely no longer the case. UML is just one of many modeling languages specified by the OMG. UML is primarily targeted for modeling software architecture and design, which is an important part, but still only a subset of what comprises an enterprise architecture.

3.2. *Service-oriented architecture Modeling Language (SoaML)*

The Service-oriented architecture Modeling Language (SoaML) specification [OMG 2009f] defines a UML profile and a metamodel for the design of services within a service-oriented architecture.

The goals of SoaML are to support the activities of service modeling and design and to fit into an overall model-driven development approach. The SoaML profile defines extensions to UML to support the range of modeling requirements for service-oriented architectures, including the specification of systems of services, the specification of individual service interfaces, and the specification of service implementations. This is done in such a way as to support the automatic generation of derived artefacts following an MDA based approach.

3.3. *Ontology Definition Metamodel (ODM)*

The Ontology Definition Metamodel (ODM) specification [OMG 2009g] defines a set of metamodels that represent formal logic languages such as Descriptive Logics (DL), other structural and descriptive representations such as RDF and

OWL, and also traditional software engineering languages such as UML and Entity Relationship (ER). The ODM specification offers a number of benefits to potential users, including options in the level of expressivity, grounding in formal logic, profiles and mappings to support model exchange, and providing a basis for integrating MDA and Semantic Web technologies.

3.4. *Information Management Metamodel (IMM)*

The Information Management Metamodel (IMM) RFP [OMG 2005] solicits proposals for a standard metamodel to address the needs of information management. This includes the scope of the existing Common Warehouse Metamodel (CWM) standard [OMG 2003]. Using CWM, developers can generate specific data models, including relational tables, records, structures and XML database designs. The ongoing work on IMM will be an extensive revision to CWM.

4. Conclusion

In this paper we have given an overview of selected OMG modeling standard initiatives that we see relevant for Enterprise Interoperability in the context of enterprise architecture. The selected standards have been positioned in the Zachman Framework (see Figure 1) to illustrate the coverage of the OMG specifications with respect to enterprise architecture. OMG should be regarded as an important industry consortium that standardizes and promotes many relevant specifications to support interoperability. One important benefit of using OMG standards is that all standards are based on the common modeling infrastructure MOF, which ensures that the models are tied together in an overall architecture. This has the advantage that tools and methodologies that are based on OMG standards will be able to exchange models and interpret the different models.

The work presented here has mainly been done in the 7th Framework Programme research project [SHAPE] (ICT-2007-216408). The project has been closely involved in the development of the SoaML specification. The overall aim of SHAPE is to develop the foundations for the model-driven development of service-oriented system landscapes with support for the integration of other technologies in order to increase the effectiveness and quality of modern software and system engineering.

5. References

[BEI] BEI, "Business Ecology Initiative", Object Management Group. http://www.business-ecology.org/ (accessed: 2010).

[Department of Defense] Department of Defense, "The DoDAF Architecture Framework Version 2.0", Department of Defense. http://cio-nii.defense.gov/sites/dodaf20/index.html (accessed: 2010).

[Li, *et al.* 2006] M.-S. Li, R. Cabral, G. Doumeingts, and K. Popplewell, "Enterprise Interoperability Research Roadmap, Final Version, Version 4.0", July 2006.

[MDA] MDA, "Model Driven Architecture", Object Management Group. http://www.omg.org/mda/ (accessed: 2010).

[Ministry of Defence] Ministry of Defence, "MOD Architecture Framework (MODAF)", Ministry of Defence. http://www.mod.uk/DefenceInternet/AboutDefence/WhatWeDo/InformationManagement/MODAF/ (accessed: 2010).

[OMG 2003] OMG, "Common Warehouse Metamodel (CWM) Specification, Version 1.1, Volume 1", Object Management Group, OMG Document formal/03-03-02, March 2003. http://www.omg.org/spec/CWM/1.1/PDF/

[OMG 2004] OMG, "Organization Structure Metamodel (OSM) Request For Proposal", Object Management Group, OMG Document bei/04-06-05, 2004. http://www.omg.org/cgi-bin/doc?bei/04-06-05.pdf

[OMG 2005] OMG, "Request for Proposal Information Management Metamodel (IMM)", Object Management Group, OMG Document ab/05-12-02, 2005. http://www.omg.org/cgi-bin/doc?ab/05-12-02.pdf

[OMG 2006] OMG, "Meta Object Facility (MOF) Core Specification, Version 2.0", Object Management Group, OMG Document formal/06-01-01, January 2006. http://www.omg.org/spec/MOF/2.0/PDF/

[OMG 2008a] OMG, "Business Motivation Model, Version 1.0", Object Management Group, OMG Document formal/2008-08-02, August 2008a. http://www.omg.org/spec/BMM/1.0/PDF/

[OMG 2008b] OMG, "Semantics of Business Vocabulary and Business Rules (SBVR), version 1.0", Object Management Group, OMG Document formal/2008-01-02, January 2008b. http://www.omg.org/spec/SBVR/1.0/PDF/

[OMG 2009a] OMG, "Business Process Model and Notation (BPMN), FTF Beta 1 for Version 2.0", Object Management Group, OMG Document dtc/2009-08-14, August 2009a. http://www.omg.org/spec/BPMN/2.0/Beta1/PDF/

[OMG 2009b] OMG, "Value Delivery Metamodel (VDM) Request For Proposal", Object Management Group, OMG Document bmi/2009-03-09, 2009b. http://www.omg.org/cgi-bin/doc?bmi/09-03-09.pdf

[OMG 2009c] OMG, "Case Management Process Modeling (CMPM) Request For Proposal", Object Management Group, OMG Document bmi/09-09-23, 2009c. http://www.omg.org/cgi-bin/doc?bmi/09-09-23.pdf

[OMG 2009d] OMG, "OMG Unified Modeling Language (OMG UML), Infrastructure, Version 2.2", Object Management Group, OMG Document formal/2009-02-04, February 2009d. http://www.omg.org/spec/UML/2.2/Infrastructure/PDF/

[OMG 2009e] OMG, "OMG Unified Modeling Language (OMG UML), Superstructure, Version 2.2", Object Management Group, OMG Document formal/2009-02-02, February 2009e. http://www.omg.org/spec/UML/2.2/Superstructure/PDF/

[OMG 2009f] OMG, "Service oriented architecture Modeling Language (SoaML), FTF Beta 1", Object Management Group, OMG Document ptc/2009-04-01, April 2009f. http://www.omg.org/spec/SoaML/1.0/Beta1/PDF/

[OMG 2009g] OMG, "Ontology Definition Metamodel, Version 1.0", Object Management Group, OMG Document formal/2009-05-01, May 2009g. http://www.omg.org/spec/ODM/1.0/PDF

[The Open Group] The Open Group, "The Open Group arcitectural framework (TOGAF), Version 9", The Open Group. http://www.opengroup.org/togaf/ (accessed: 2010).

[Zachman 1987] J. A. Zachman, "A Framework for Information Systems Architecture", IBM Systems Journal, vol. 26, no. 3, 1987. http://www.research.ibm.com/journal/50th/applications/zachman.html

Standards Creation and Adoption for SME Networks

The Experience of the European Textile-Clothing and Footwear Industry

Piero De Sabbata* — Nicola Gessa* — Arianna Brutti* — Cristiano Novelli* — Angelo Frascella* — Gianluca D'Agosta*

*ENEA,
Via Martiri di Monte Sole, 4
40129 Bologna
Italy
piero.desabbata@enea.it
nicola.gessa@enea.it
arianna.brutti@enea.it
cristiano.novelli@enea.it
angelo.frascella@enea.it
gianluca.dagosta@enea.it

ABSTRACT. *This paper presents the experience that is running in the Textile, Clothing and Footwear industry under the framework of the European project eBIZ-TCF as a case of standardization in industrial sectors that are characterized by the large presence of SMEs. The activities are presented in connection with previous initiatives that constitute the industrial and technological background of such initiative. In fact it is a long way that leaded the actors of the project to identify the requirements and remove the bottlenecks that hamper eBusiness adoption in a crucial part of the European manufacturing industry.*

KEYWORDS: *eBusiness, standards, networked business, Textile Clothing Industry, ebXML, UBL, SME*

1. Introduction

In January 2009 an independent group, the Expert Panel for the Review of the European Standardisation System (EXPRESS) was established by the European Commission. Its aim was to review the entire European Standardisation System (ESS) in the European 2020 perspective.

As a first statement the report, released on February 2010 (Express, 10), declares "The ESS has been a central element in the delivery of the single European market, in particular, through the use of Directives in key areas under the 'New Approach' policy, integrated into the New Legislative Framework."

Then, as one of the final recommendations, the expert groups points out the need "to promote a coherent work program where there is ease of access for all interested stakeholders, such as SMEs, to standardization work and standards information."

These statements are the most recent ones in a sequence of reports, positions papers, political statements regarding the role of standardization, the importance of the involvement of industry (especially SMEs) at general and sectorial level and the need for the European economy to exploit the opportunities offered by the technology (and the new ways to do business they can enable).

An important statement about the relevance of sector specific actions addressing SMEs is also witnessed by content of the "CEN/ISSS ROADMAP addressing key eBusiness standards issues 2003-2005" (Kuster *et al.*, 2003).

Despite this importance and its necessity still eBusiness is far from a wide diffusion in the networks of European industry, especially in sectors dominated by a large presence of SMEs. For example Textile, Clothing and Footwear (TCF) sectors show an average level of adoption of eBusiness and interoperability standards that appears to be quite lower comparing to other similar manufacturing sectors (ebWatch, 04, ebWatch 05). Other sectors characterized by the large presence of SMEs and the absence of few preeminent leaders, like furniture, are not so far from this picture.

It is not in our focus in this paper to discuss the reasons why a wide eBusiness adoption should be desirable and how it would benefit our industry. But to understand how and why the problem of interoperability has hampered standard adoption and how the standardization processes have been tackled in order to overcome the low level of adaption in respect of other sectors.

2. Factors hampering eBusiness diffusion in TCF

An analysis report recently published by the eBIZ-TCF project (eBIZ, 08) has shown evidence of some aspects of the problem that can be resumed in:

– Sectorial specific requirements: intercompany relationships based on multiple connections in a *m to n* schema instead of a *1 to n* schema, production processes largely sector specific and demanding for sector specific solutions, inconstant relationships on a seasonal basis.

– Technological offer for eBusiness implementation: existence of a number of solutions and initiatives (implementing different paradigms: P2P as well as Web Application based and Integration Services) but with a very low level of adoption and no capacity to interoperate each other (they are islands of interoperability, not interconnected).

– eBusiness adoption is hampered by:

  - insufficient perceived benefits;

  - lacking interoperability between different solutions conflicts with the high dynamicity of the *m to n* relationships;

  - differences at the business level, including not only the content of data messages but also the organization of business processes.

On the contrary, this is the evaluation from the report, the existence of numerous solutions and (some) standards does not present the biggest single obstacle to eBusiness adoption because at the technical level, different standards do not necessarily prevent interoperation between different systems.

A reluctance was observed of many firms and technology providers to implement common specifications, fearing a risk of an excessive "normalization" of the applications that leads to loss of their assets towards the customers or their suppliers; they instead wait and see which will be the successful initiative when the risk on investing will be lowered to zero.

On the other hand, from concrete practices, it was also observed that even the pressure from large industry to activate electronic data flows might be unsuccessful because suppliers are not convinced to invest in a single customer solution; this puts in evidence a request for common languages and standards to preserve IT and organizational investments (DeSabbata *et al.*, 2008).

The need for standardized solutions is strengthened by the high volatility of the commercial relationships in the sector: the fashion waves and the market evolution leads us to change yearly a relevant part of the partners.

In short, the perceived negative key factors for the SME networks in the textile clothing and footwear sector could be resumed in:

– high threshold to begin the eBusiness "game";

– difficulty in setting up/understanding collaboration processes;

– long time in setting up and testing the network;

– costly scaling.

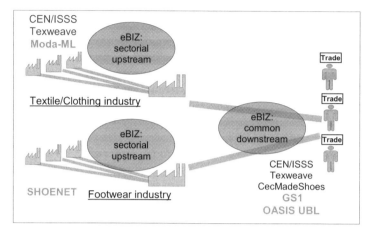

Figure 1. *The eBIZ-TCF architecture in short*

These statements depict a situation where interoperability appears to be a key issue for eBusiness adoption and the adoption of standards plays a relevant role in four key aspects: a) lowering the investment for each firm to participate in the "game"; b) achieving a longer life time of the adopted IT solutions; c) offering a reference state of art as a benchmark for collaborative processes to be implemented; d) increasing perceived benefits thanks to a larger number of adopters (that are partners technically ready to collaborate).

3. Criticalities in achieving interoperability and standard contribution

In order to establish interoperability between different systems there are at least three aspects of interoperability that must be tackled:

– business processes;

– data models (semantic, syntax, including product classification and identification);

– communication protocols.

The analysis in the TCF sectors demonstrated that the communication protocols are not affected by sector specific issues and are not so critical, because the outcomes of IT research and developments from other applicative domains can be applied directly, with no adaptation (but with a clear understanding of costs and functionalities that fit the technological level of each organization).

On the contrary, business processes and data models are very sector specific and attempts to directly transfer tools and solutions from other sectors have proved to be unsuccessful. This is the reason why in the TCF sector there has been constant attention to these two aspects of interoperability.

More in detail, since the beginning the work of analysis (Texspin 04, DeSabbata *et al.* 2008) leaded to identify two different challenges related to the requisites of the different rings of the supply chains of the TCF industry (Figure 1):

– highly specialized networks of manufacturing enterprises (upstream area) where very sector-specific (vertical) languages (and data models) have to be provided (DeSabbata et al., 2005a, 2005b);

– retail channels for the final goods (downstream area) where normalization and common and efficient connections are required by the retailers to the producers of different sectors (thus non-sector-specific, horizontal languages).

On the other hand difficulties in participating in standardization processes were immediately clear for a sector dominated by SMEs (DeSabbata *et al.*, 2005a, Jakobs 04):

– time: the life-cycles in the standardization processes are too long;

– resources: the extent of human and economical resources prevent SMEs participation;

– usability: the specifications have poor usability (address few expert readers);

– adoption: the integration in legacy systems/ERPs requires specific technological skills;

– implementation complexity: the complexity of the software to implement the full specifications is costly and often not incremental.

In order to tackle these issues, both Textile-Clothing and Footwear sectors, in parallel, de facto adopted a "light" approach to the creation of a standardized interoperability framework (DeSabbata *et al. 2008*, Gessa *et al.*, 2005) with the following requirements:

– user driven: a bottom-up approach involving relevant actors since the beginning, on local small tasks at a time;

– sectorial: focused on a narrow domain but aware of horizontal frameworks (like ebXML or UBL);

– dictionary centric rather than document centric: in order to reuse terms in many document templates with reduced time to deliver usable results;

– supported by public specifications and on-line free resources;

– iterative: the starting point is a core of inter-company processes; they are analyzed and implemented with the support of a group of pilot industries and then proposed in a standardization framework; then further iteration consolidates and extends the existing dictionaries and specifications; the CEN/ISSS CWA approach has been an enabling factor for the success of this strategy.

The result of such an approach has been a sequence of independently promoted initiatives that, *de facto,* implemented an iterative standardization lifecycle (see

Figure 2, Gessa *et al.*, 2005): after the first initiatives in 1990s (EDITEX, result of TEDIS project, TEDIS 92), the two industry associations, Euratex and CEC, jointly with EU Commission, CEN/ISSS and others actors like GS1 and ENEA promoted TexWeave for Textile/Clothing (TexWeave 05), CEN/ISSS FINEC for Footwear (EFNET 03, EFNET 05). In the meantime a number of "user centric" demonstration initiatives and projects (like eTexML, Visit, Moda-ML, EFNET2/3, CecMadeShoe, ShoeNet, TQR, IPSA, etc.) with a wide involvement of industry associations, prepared a background of analysis and specifications that was (almost) ready to be implemented by the industry.

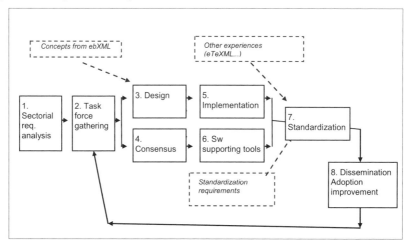

Figure 2. *The textile-clothing standardization lifecycle (Gessa et al., 2005)*

4. The role of research for standards, the role of standards for research

It is worth mentioning that, in parallel, the NMP Leapfrog Integrated Project (www.leapfrog-eu.org) had activities to provide new tools and methodologies to implement the concept of the Extended Smart Garment Organization (xSGO) model in the Textile/Clothing sector (Artschwager *et al.*, 2009) with the following objectives:

– reduction of misalignment between different organizations by managing models of the collaboration processes and agreements;

– fast setup of collaborative procedures and customized data models.

For inter-organizational data flows, a shared semantics was derived from standard specifications (Moda-ML/TexWeave, ebXML) and a methodology and tools were developed to facilitate their adoption.

The outcome of this work was Knowledge Exchange Infrastructure (KEI), a conceptual framework supported by artefacts, software tools and a sectorial ontology (OntoModa) that, subsequently, has been published (www.moda-ml.org/moda-ml/Ontologies/Moda-ML/ModaMLOntology.owl) to support both semantic reconciliation applications as well as document (re-)engineering (DeSabbata *et al.*, 2009).

The integration of technological and organizational aspects while building enterprise networks and the creation of open communities that exploit standardization outcomes is an achievement of LeapFrog IP. Thus the contribution from Leapfrog to the subsequent standardization initiatives (like eBIZ-TCF) can be resumed in:

– collaboration architecture as an open, non monolithic, composition of different contributions (methods, resources, solutions) at different levels, partially public and partially intrinsically proprietary;

– networks of firms as systems of stakeholders with different roles and drivers;

– KEI tools to simplify the definition of e-Business collaborations and to release artifacts and resources.

Similar initiatives, more focused on business processes and communication architecture were managed in parallel in the Footwear sector, CecMadeShoes project (www.cec-made-shoe.com), for example (Chituc 2008a, Chituc 2008b).

5. The role of eBIZ-TCF, an eBusiness harmonization initiative

At the end of this path, in 2008, a new large scale initiative was launched to foster the adoption of eBusiness jointly (for the first time) in Textile-Clothing (TC) and Footwear (FW) though the call for tender "Harmonising eBusiness processes and data exchanges for SMEs in the Textile/Clothing and Footwear sectors in the Single Market" issued by DG Enterprise & Industry.

A consortium promoted by Euratex (coordinator, Textile/Clothing industry European association), CEC (Footwear industry European association) and ENEA in collaboration with GS1 and Hermes Lab answered with the eBIZ-TCF project (eBusiness for Textile/Clothing and Footwear, www.ebiz-tcf.eu).

The first objective of the project was to systematize existing standards and experiences through the definition of a Reference Architecture for eBusiness in the textile/clothing and footwear sectors; it tackles distinctly downstream and upstream requirements for the supply chain with appropriate technological and methodological specifications related to data models, communication protocols and product classification:

– upstream, distinct sectorial business models and languages (Moda-ML, Shoenet);

– downstream, common use profiles for a generic eBusiness language (UBL) and adoption of product and party identification standards (GS1 GTIN and GLN).

The second objective has been to demonstrate the suitability of the Architecture for the sectors and obtain consensus from the stakeholders. During the project, a public call received applications for pilots and, in the end, 17 were accepted with more than 150 organizations across 20 European countries (DeSabbata *et al.*, 2008, see Figure 3).

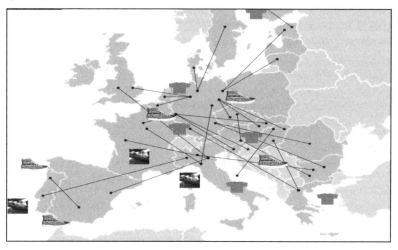

Figure 3. *Map of eBIZ-TCF pilots across Europe (list on the website)*

In order to meet the requirements for interoperability in SMEs networks the project focused on three aspects:

– clear, free, easy-to-use documentation of the specifications (targeting different potential types of users) and the availability of a set of related public resources (XML Schema, XSL, samples, technical user guides, use profiles, tools, economical benefit studies) and related tools for automatic documentation creation/ maintenance/change management (eBIZ 09);

– adoption of use profiles and strict typing to reduce Redundancy and Uncertainty in the specifications in order to reduce the efforts: a) to map internal processes and data models towards the specifications, b) to reconcile different implementations of the same specifications. A first method to measure these parameters has been proposed (Brutti *et al.*, 2010);

– clear identification of the different layers of decisions (Figure 4) that are necessary to reduce Redundancy and Uncertainty in the implementation: from the general standard model (UBL) to the sectorial use profile (eBIZ-TCF) to the inter-company agreement (firms through ebXML) (Brutti *et al.*, 2010).

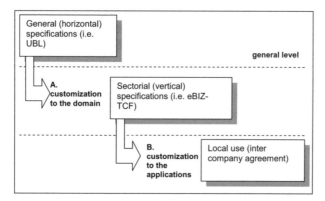

Figure 4. *Different layers of decision and specialization/customization (from Brutti et al., 2010)*

6. Conclusions: lessons learnt and the outlook

The methodologies for checking and self-evaluation during both the Use Profiles creation/maintenance process as well as during their implementation by the developers emerged as a relevant open issue, that eBIZ-TCF has only begun to tackle (Brutti 2010).

On the other hand, for the first time, thanks to the common effort of many actors (associations, European Commission, technology suppliers and research organizations) there is an architecture in place that is open and "standard-aware" and with a large number of adopters all around Europe; finally some lessons have been learnt:

– large scale adoptions of standards requires the contribution of a plurality of actors (industry associations, researchers, service or technology suppliers) when the presence of SMEs is predominant; unilateral actions cannot build a sectorial reference architecture (or application);

– specific sectorial requirements and skills availability are relevant in the implementation of standards and of interoperability technologies; that requires a relationships between technologies and industrial policies fostering their adoption;

– a virtuous cyclic interaction between standardization, research and technology uptake activities can benefit the capacity of industry to achieve their goals in the game of standardization;

– the issues of customization and validation with "light" tools and procedures are still open.

7. References

[Artschwager *et al.*, 2009] A. Artschwager, T. Fischer, D. Stellmach. "New quality of partnership in the Textile World Concepts and Technologies", in *Transforming Clothing Production into a Demand Driven, Knowledge-based High Tech Industry, the Leapfrog Paradigm*, edited by Lutz Walter, George-Alexander Kartsounis, Stefano Carosio, Springer Verlag, London, 2009.

[Brutti *et al.*, 2010] A. Brutti, V. Cerminara, S. Cristiani, P. De Sabbata, N. Gessa, "Use profile management for standard conformant customisation", *I-ESA 2010*, to be published.

[Chituc *et al.*, 2008a] C.M. Chituc, C. Toscano, A. Azevedo, "Interoperability in collaborative networks: independent and industry-specific initiatives – The case of the footwear industry", *Computers in Industry,* special issue on *Enterprise Integration and Interoperability In Manufacturing Systems*, vol. 59, no. 7, pp. 741-757. 2008.

[Chituc *et al.*, 2008b] C.M. Chituc, A. Azevedo, C. Toscano (2008), "An Analytical Approach for Comparing Business Frameworks", in *Innovation in Manufacturing Networks, Eighth IFIP International Conference on Information Technology for Balanced Automation Systems*, BASYS 2008, Porto, Portugal, June 23-25, 2008, (Ed. Azevedo, Américo), IFIP International Federation for Information Processing, Springer, vol. 266, pp. 137-144.

[DeSabbata *et al.*, 2005a] P. De Sabbata, N. Gessa, C. Novelli, A. Frascella, F. Vitali, "B2B: Standardisation or Customisation?", pp 1556-1566, in *Innovation and the Knowledge Economy Issues, Application, Case Studies*, e-Challenges 2005 conference, Ljubljiana, October 19-21 2005, edited by Paul Cunningham and Miriam Cunningham, IIMC International Information Management Corporation LTD, Dublin, Ireland, IOS Press.

[DeSabbata *et al.*, 2005b] P. De Sabbata, N. Gessa, G. Cucchiara, T. Imolesi, F. Vitali, "Supporting eBusiness with a dictionary designed in a vertical standardisation perspective", in *Proceedings of IEEE CEC 2005, 7th International IEEE Conference on E-Commerce Technology*, Monaco 19-22 July 2005, published by the IEEE Computer Society Press.

[DeSabbata *et al.*, 2008] P. De Sabbata, M. Scalia, M. Baker, J. Somers, M. Stefanova, A. Brutti, A. Frascella, "eBIZ-TCF: an initiative to improve eAdoption in European Textile/Clothing and Footwear industry", in *Proceedings of e-Challenges 2008 conference*, Stockholm, October 22-24 2008, pp. 1169-1180, edited by Paul Cunningham and Miriam Cunningham, IIMC International Information Management Corporation LTD, Dublin, Ireland, IOS Press.

[DeSabbata *et al.*, 2009] P. De Sabbata, N. Gessa, G. D'Agosta, M. Busanelli, C. Novelli, "Knowledge Exchange Infrastructure to Support Extended Smart Garment Organizations", in *Transforming Clothing Production into a Demand Driven, Knowledge-based High Tech Industry, the Leapfrog Paradigm*, edited by Lutz Walter, George-Alexander Kartsounis, Stefano Carosio, Springer Verlag, London, 2009.

[eBIZ 08] eBIZ-TCF Project, "Analysis report on eBusiness adoption in Textile/Clothing and Footwear sectors", Project deliverable D2.1, Brussels, June 2008, http://wp1107496.wp142.webpack.hosteurope.de/sitemgr-site/files/Analysis_report_on_eBusiness_adoption_v2.1.pdf

[eBIZ 09] eBIZ-TCF Project, "Reference Architecture for eBusiness harmonisation in Textile/Clothing and Footwear sectors", Project deliverable D3.5, Brussels, December 2009. http://www.ebiz-tcf.eu/sitemgr-site/files/OF510-010-V1-Reference %20architecture %20-%20pdf.zip

[ebWatch 04] e-Business w@tch, "electronic Business in the Textile, Clothing and Footwear industries", *sector report n. 01-11*, Brussels, August 2004, www.ebusiness-watch.org/studies/sectors/textile_clothing/documents/Textile_2005.pdf

[ebWatch 05] e-Business w@tch, "e-Business interoperability and standards-A cross sectorial perspective and outlook", Special report, Brussels, September 2005

[EFNET, 03] EFNET-2, FINEC, "Electronic Commerce: A case study of the footwear industry in Europe" *CEN/ISSS CWA 14746:2003*, CEN/ISSS, June 2003, Brussels.

[EFNET, 04] EFNET-3, FINEC, "Proposal for an XML based format for storage and exchange of design data in the footwear industry", *CEN/ISSS CWA 15043:2004(E)*, July 2004, Brussels.

[Express 10] Express Group. "Standardization For A Competitive And Innovative Europe: A Vision For 2020", *Report Of The Expert Panel For The Review Of The European Standardization System*, February 2010, http://ec.europa.eu/enterprise/policies/european-standards/files/express/exp_384_express_report_final_distrib_en.pdf

[Gessa *et al.*, 05] N. Gessa, G. Cucchiara, P. De Sabbata, A. Brutti, "A bottom-up approach to build a B2B sectorial standard: the case of Moda-ML/TexSpin", pp 249-260, in *Interoperability of Enterprise Software Applications*, workshops of the INTEROP-ESA International Conference, Geneva 22 February 2005, edited by Hervé Panetto, Hermes Science Publishing, Paris, 2005.

[Jakobs 04] K. Jakobs, "Standardisation and SME Users Mutually Exclusive?", *Proc. Multi-Conference on Business Information Systems*, Cuvillier Verlag, 2004

[Kuster *et al.*, 2003] M.W.Kuster, Man Tse Li, B.Gatti, "CEN/ISSS report and recommendations on key eBusiness standards issues 2003-2005", report of CEN/ISSS eBIF forum, 2003 CEN

[TEDIS 92] TEDIS, Trade EDI Systems Programme, "Interim report", 1992, *Office for Official Publications of the European Community*.

[Texspin 04] TexSpin, "TexSpin, Guidelines for XML/EDI messages in the Textile/Clothing sector", *CEN/ISSS CWA 14948:2004*, March 2004, Brussels.

[TexWeave 06] TexWeave, "TexWeave: Scenarios and XML templates for B2B in the textile clothing manufacturing and retail", *CEN/ISSS CWA 15557:2006*, 2006, Brussels; http://www.texweave.org.

The European Public Procurement Initiative and Standards for Information Exchange

Tim McGrath

Document Engineering Services
PO Box 1289
Fremantle WA 6160
Australia
tim.mcgrath@documentengineeringservices.com

ABSTRACT. *The Pan-European Public eProcurement On-Line (PEPPOL) project is an initiative to align business processes for eProcurement across all Government Agencies within Europe.*

The approach taken follows the European Interoperability Framework, focusing on the transport, semantic and organizational factors. Rather than attempt to create new standards in these areas, the project has chosen to create implementation sets or profiles of existing standards. The transport protocol, BusDox, is a profile for using Web Service standards. The semantic and organizational rules are from the CEN/ISSS Business Interoperability Interfaces (CEN/BII) workshop.

This paper outlines the PEPPOL project, the standards themselves, and the governance issues that result from this approach.

1. Introduction

The Pan-European Public eProcurement On-Line (PEPPOL)[1] project is a European Commission Large Scale Pilot to align business processes for eProcurement between economic operators and Government Agencies across Europe.

The approach taken follows the European Interoperability Framework, focusing on the transport, semantic and organizational factors. Rather than attempt to create new standards in these areas, the project has chosen to create implementation sets or profiles of existing standards. The transport protocol, BusDox, is a profile for using OASIS[2] standards. The semantic and organizational rules are from the CEN/ISSS Business Interoperability Interfaces workshop (CEN/BII)[3]. In effect, PEPPOL is creating implementation guides for the use of these standards in public eProcurement.

This approach to ensuring common implementation of standards results in governance issues for the long-term sustainability of the services developed.

2. Public eProcurement

Government agencies are the largest buyer in the European Union and account for around 16% of GDP, which is equal to 1,500 Billion Euro. However this purchasing power is not distributed evenly across member states. In many cases physical borders have been replaced by technical borders. As part of its Competitiveness and Innovation Programme[4] the European Commission is seeking ways to remove these technical barriers to cross border eProcurement through the PEPPOL project.

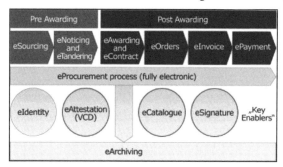

Figure 1. *Scope of PEPPOL processes for Public Procurement*

---

1 http://www.peppol.eu.
2 http://www.oasis-open.org.
3 http://spec.cenbii.eu/.
4 http://ec.europa.eu/cip/.

The broader vision of PEPPOL is that any company (including small enterprises) in the EU can communicate electronically with any EU governmental institution for the entire post-award procurement processes. PEPPOL also partially supports pre-award processes by providing services and standards for qualification evidences for attestation (also known as the Virtual Company Dossier) and pre-award product catalogues.

In this way, the PEPPOL project pilots will allow any economic operator in the EU and the European Economic Area (EEA) to respond electronically to any published public tender notice and any subsequent purchasing processes.

Of course, there is no difference between post-award procurement for the public and private sector so what we envision is an entire European eProcurement community connected by PEPPOL standards and at the same time creating a single window to European procurement processes for non-European organizations.

3. Interoperability through PEPPOL

There are many barriers to the open exchange of business information for Public eProcurement, not all of which can be addressed by projects such as PEPPOL. Figure 2 shows how PEPPOL is addressing the Semantic, Technical and Organizational barriers using the European Interoperability Framework[5] as a reference model. The Legal barriers are being addressed by other EC initiatives and PEPPOL will provide input into those.

	Barriers	Solutions
Organizational	• Business requirements vary a lot • No agreed upon businesses processes • Huge difference in business models	• Mandate minimal business processes • Set-up a well defined governance process
Legal	• High barriers in previous legislation • Member states implement directives differently	• Multilateral peering agreement • Loosen technical requirements • Align MS implementation of directives
Semantic	• Different data models • Different coding systems • No common understanding	• Define mandatory set of data-elements • Promote common standards • Accept syntax mappings will co-exist
Technical	• Incompatible technical solutions • Shared infrastructure components are missing	• Mandate a transport standard • Establish and fund core infrastructure

Figure 2. *PEPPOL solutions for interoperability with Public eProcurement*

---

5 http://ec.europa.eu/idabc/en/document/3473.

As can be seen in Figure 2, the solutions to these barriers are being addressed in part by using open standards.

3.1. *Standards for the PEPPOL transport infrastructure*

Building from the successful experience of the Danish NemHandel project[6], PEPPOL is creating a "four-corner model" for secure and reliable exchange of electronic documents. By "four-corner" we mean a protocol for interconnecting the various established islands of networks currently used for European eProcurement.

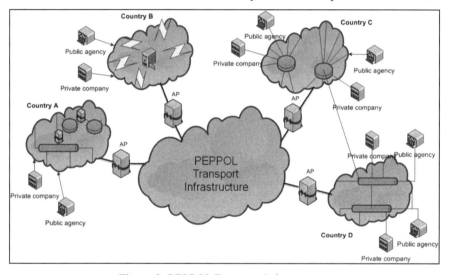

Figure 3. *PEPPOL Transport Infrastructure*

This model supports the overall design targets which were that national or extant solutions will not be replaced but linked through a common infrastructure based on open standards.

The transport infrastructure used for PEPPOL is known as BusDox (derived from **Bu**siness **Do**cument e**X**change network). BusDox does not attempt to replace existing messaging service standards instead it provides a simplified interface independent of the various standards used for the exchange of documents.

By nature of its design, Busdox is not specific to eProcurement, it is a generic protocol for secure and reliable messaging useful for any electronic document exchanges. It is already being considered for other European Commission services.

---

6 http://www.nemhandel.dk/#/forside.

3.2. *PEPPOL semantic standards*

For its common semantics PEPPOL is implementing a series of business processes using the profiles created by the CEN/ISSS BII (Business Interoperability Interfaces for Public procurement in Europe) workshop.

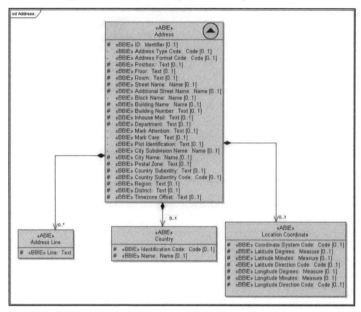

Figure 4. *BII structures for Business Information Entities*

The BII profile specifications include transaction data models of the documents exchanged together with their requisite elements (known as Business Information Entities). For example, Figure 4 illustrates the logical structure for the components of an address. These transaction data models may be bound to different syntactical representations. In PEPPOL's case, there are mappings to both OASIS UBL[7] and UN/CEFACT[8] syntaxes.

3.3. *Business process standards*

A BII profile also defines the business processes and the exchanges of documents between two business parties. Figure 5 illustrates the hierarchy of definitions within a BII profile.

---

7 http://www.oasis-open.org/committees/tc_home.php?wg_abbrev=ubl.
8 http://www.unece.org/cefact/.

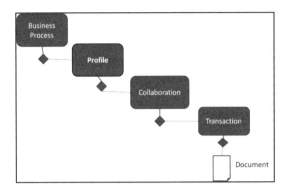

Figure 5. *BII Profile Architecture*

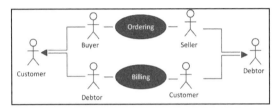

Figure 6. *BII Profiles for Simple Procurement*

By way of illustration, Figure 6 describes the use case for Simple Procurement business process within the BII specifications.

3.4. *BII Profiles used within PEPPOL*

Not all possible BII profiles are used by the initial implementations of PEPPOL. Based on the scope (see Figure 1) a selected group of profiles are being used. These are listed in Table 1.

Virtual Company Dossier Submission
VCD Packaging
Catalogue Request
BII01 Catalogue Only
BII18 Punch out
BII03 Basic Order Only
BII04 Basic Invoice Only
BII05 Basic Billing
BII06 Basic Procurement
BII07 Simple Procurement

Table 1. *BII Profiles implemented by PEPPOL*

4. Governance of standards used by PEPPOL

Any project implementing standards for eProcurement will require services and tools to manage the governance of their customizations and implementations. For example, the standards governance for PEPPOL must keep the data exchange standards in a form that will not be altered without the user community consent. It must also provide support materials such as:

– a standardized reference model for all implementations;

– a recommended implementation process within a community of users, identifying the relationships between all parties to the governance package and the cooperation needed between them to realize the full benefits of adoption;

– a requirement to adopt open standards that not only promote integration with other services but also capture "data coherence" and "semantic consistency" of the information between these services;

– a standards-based conformance model that can also be used to pre-qualify incoming participants and set required levels of engagement as dictated by the governance model.

The term governance has been deliberately chosen to encompass the scope of this responsibility. Governance has been defined as "rules, processes and behavior that affect the way in which powers are exercised.... particularly as regards openness, participation, accountability, effectiveness and coherence"[9].

Standards implementation governance is the way in which decisions important for the implementation of a standard are taken, communicated, monitored and assessed. In PEPPOL we are particularly concerned about the decisions important to the interoperability of the XML documents exchanged in electronic business processes. The PEPPOL project is designed to continue after the initial project concludes in November 2011. Negotiations are underway for the infrastructure and services themselves to be transferred to more permanent agencies within the European Commission itself. This means that the implementations of the various standards involved also need to be sustainable into the future. Therefore, it has been decided to transfer this responsibility away from governmental agencies and towards two standard development organizations, OASIS and CEN.

4.1. *Governance of BusDox*

A Technical Committee is being established within the OASIS consortium to provide the governance necessary for the BusDox specifications.

---

9 European Commission, European Governance – A White Paper, 2001.

The purpose of the BusDox TC is to define, enhance and maintain profiles of existing standards (from OASIS and elsewhere) that specify interfaces for a lightweight and federated messaging infrastructure supporting secure and reliable exchange of electronic documents.

4.2. *Governance of BII standards*

The forum for continued development and governance of the BII deliverables will be the newly-formed CEN/BII2 workshop.

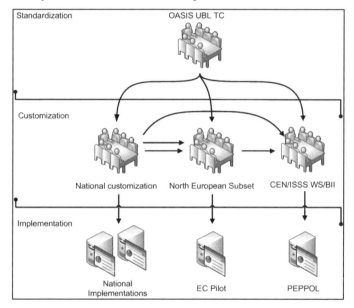

Figure 7. *Governance Hierarchy for PEPPOL business processes*

5. Summary

Any organization or project implementing open standards for document exchange needs to not only consider the ongoing governance of those standards but also the governance of the implementation guides that relate to the use of those standards in their specific context of use.

Within PEPPOL, the technical layer standards are expressed as the BusDox profiles and the semantic and business process standards as the BII profiles.

However, PEPPOL does not intend to provide governance of these profiles. This role is best suited to *specialized* standards bodies such as OASIS and CEN.

Challenges in Project Management

Georgios Kapogiannis* — Colin Piddington**

* THINKlab, Future Workspaces Research Centre
University of Salford
UK
G.Kapogiannis@salford.ac.uk

** TANet/CONTROL2K
C.Piddington@cimmedia.com

ABSTRACT. *The challenges to business will always increase as long as organizational and project procedures are unsuccessful. This situation forces directors and managers to act by making ineffectual decisions which reflect the organizational and project progress either in the short or long term. This paper aims to bring these challenges into consideration by improving and enhancing the decisional quality. A workshop held at the University of Salford – THINKlab – attempted to address these challenges and to translate them into future needs to enhance the competitive capabilities of the UK in the global market place. For this purpose, directors and managers from the construction, automotive and aerospace industry were invited to attend, as these represent a difference in IT maturity and the use of resources. The contribution of academia towards this target is key due to the innovative capabilities that are being researched. One of the results of this workshop was that industry and academia are not collaborative enough. It was also clear that the experts do not share their own ideas or documents due to the lack of trust and the feeling that knowledge is power. The result is a weak partnership schema and also a lack of contribution towards new ideas or products, i.e. low innovation. All these have been characterized as challenges that have to be considered and improved, targeting new business ideas – products or services – leading to more efficient project progress and control.*

KEYWORDS: *collaborative environment, business environment, project management, investments on information and communication technologies*

1. Introduction

The center of the workshop discussion focused on the need to enable the capability of being more competent, in terms of using human capital as well as technology and appropriate management processes. Experience tells us that machines/ processes are satisfactory when they work. However, when things deviate from the known processes (breakdowns and other unforeseen occurrences) we have to send people to the rescue to ensure the business is not affected. Process complexity today is on the increase due to different working practices across organizations and the geographical location of the resources. Multiple skills and relevant applications are required all through the product/project lifecycles leading to successful missions. This exasperates the problems (Kapogiannis *et al*, 2010). This situation was discussed following presentations by industry as to the current state of the art, their experiences and their views of the future. This was then debated against a presentation of new enabling technological services to stimulate a futuristic view.

2. Exercise

At the end of the workshop participants were required to answer two questions: How do you define collaboration? What are the collaboration challenges? The answer to the first question was that collaboration in a modern economic environment of business is defined as:

> *a better team performance between stakeholders of a project, a product or a service, with its main target the better operation and further development of their business value(s) by sharing common goals (April, 2010).*

The benefits of collaboration in an economy and a modern economic environment of business were seen as those listed in Table 1.

	Benefits of Collaboration	Modern Economic Environment of Business
1.	Reduce Risks and reward	Economic
2.	Increase Market Share	Economic
3.	Access and Utilization of capital and Human Resources	Economic and Business
4.	Improving profitability and long terms sustainability	Economic and Business
5.	Developing skills	Business (Management)
6.	Enhancing Learning	Business (Management)
7.	Increase efficiency of project	Economic and Business
8.	More integrated environment	Business (Management)
9.	Problem resolution	Economic and Business (Management)
10.	Building Trust	Business (Management)

Table 1. *Benefits of collaboration in modern economic business environment*

The answers to "the challenges of collaboration" were mainly focused on the economic environment of business, making use of ICT and human behavior. Further information is listed in Table 2 to understand this better.

ICT	Human Behavior	Economic Business Environment
Collaborative Environments	Building Trust	Adopt collaboration by top management as part of the organization strategy
	Changing management culture	Efficient performance of Risk Management, Change Management and Value Management
	Improving Leadership skills and collaborative attitudes	Effective organizational readiness
	Developing manager's attitudes	Conflicts reduction and efficient problem resolution
	Inform all	Effective Partners/staff involvement
	Remove waste	Ownership business problem
	Peer pressure	Information access
	Increased responsibility	Business interoperability
	Being proactive	Reduce degree of complexity
	Being reactive	More efficient client's Requirements collection
		Reduce Cost i.e. less travel, more effective meetings (from anywhere at any time)
		Better calculation of Return of Investment (ROI)
		Better product or service design
		Better success stories

Table 2. *Challenges in an economic environment of business by the use of collaborative environments*

With regard to the above table it has to be mentioned that the human behavior impact that is developed by the use of the collaborative environment, reflects the economic business environment. The biggest challenge in human behavior is at the organizational level to make managers and project managers work together in a more proactive and reactive manner. The next section will analyze in detail the literature review of proactive behavior, which has been carried out and will end with its potential benefits in a project management environment and business environment.

2.1. *Proactive behavior and its value in dynamic management*

The dynamic view of managing projects successfully is by enhancing the skills of the project manager in the manner of controlling and making more accurate decisions. What is mainly needed in order to advance the project manager's skills is the capability to interact teamwise with the other participants or member of the organization or a project. This interaction enhances the communication and the collaboration and develops the building of trust among the project manager and the participants (Hamlin, 2008). What is more, enhancing and developing the above key elements, the outcome will efficiently create effective partnerships. The result of this attempt is to assist in reducing the degree of complexity in projects. Specifically, regarding trust, Estrin says "that innovators must trust themselves, trust the people with whom they work, and trust the people with whom they partner, balancing their progress in an environment that demands both self-doubt and self-confidence". The communication constitutes to conceptualize the processes by which people navigate and assign meaning. Communication is also understood as the exchanging of understanding. Montiel – Overall defines collaboration as "a trusting relationship between two or more equal participants involved in sharing thinking, shared planning and shared creation".

Grant and Ashford (2008) supported that in order to enhance trust, communication and collaboration the construction of the following skills is required: anticipatory, change orientation and self initiation. Henceforth these skills will lead in the development of the ProActive behavior. Additionally, he explained what proactive behavior is:

> "It is anticipatory – it involves acting in advance of a future situation, rather than just reacting. For example, the nurse has thought ahead to anticipate the doctor's needs before asked.
>
> It is change-oriented – being proactive means taking control and causing something to happen, rather than just adapting to a situation or waiting for something to happen. The production operator has caused a change before the machines are routinely changed and prevented a failure.
>
> It is self-initiated – the individual does not need to be asked to act, nor do they require detailed instructions. For example, the new management consultant in the example has not waited to be given feedback, but has proactively sought it out".

Also, Parker, Williams & Turner (2006, p. 636) defined proactive behavior as

> "self-initiated and future-oriented action that aims to change and improve the situation or oneself".

Therefore, what is needed for a more dynamic management approach is managers(s) and project(s) manager(s) to be self-initiated, future-oriented and anticipators. This behavioral situation will be used as the driving force that will initiate change in the operational and organizational system of a company. This approach will give an added value to the current state of the art in management and project management. The pro-activity concept assists managers and project managers to think before acting, during and after a meeting takes place.

3. Conclusion

The outcome of this presentation is to create a better understanding of the problems that will face an evolving business in the coming years. Industry needs managers to feel more confident with the power of collaboration, in the context of a modern economic business environment. The benefits as they are presented in Table 1 mirror the future challenges (Table 2) for both industry and academia to address as they imply new management paradigms. Managers will have to invest in Information and Communication Technologies to enable these new global processes. Academia and industry need to work together to close the gap of the lack of communication between stakeholders, and developing behaviors and skills in new business values, creating the appropriate human capital. This new human capital requires to work proactively and reactively in order to meet the current business challenges via enhanced project facilitation.

4. References

Association of Project Management (2007). APM Body of Knowledge, UK

CoSpaces, (2010) "Using Collaborative Environment and Technologies", in *Project management Life Cycle*, FP6-2007-IST -5

Gautier G., Kapogiannis.G, Piddington C., Polychronakis Y., Fernando T, *"Pro-Active Project Management"*, I-ESA China, Interoperability for Enterprise Software and Applications, 2009, IBM Conference Proceedings Publications

Grant, A. M., & Ashford, S. J. 2008. The dynamics of proactivity at work. Research in Organizational Behaviour, 28: 3-34. http://www.unc.edu/~agrant/publications.htm

Judy Estrin, *Closing the Innovation Gap: Reigniting the Spark of Creativity in a Global Economy,* New York: McGraw Hill, 2008.

Kapogiannis.G, Kagioglou M., Fernando T, Gautier G, "Enabling ProActive Behavior to future project managers", I-ESA Coventry, *Interoperability for Enterprise Software and Applications*, Springer Conference Proceedings Publications vol. V , 2010, p. 367-375

Montiel-Overall, P (2005) *Toward a Theory of Collaboration for Teachers and Librarians,* American Association of School Librarians, viewed 12 April 2010, http://www.ala.org/ala/mgrps/divs/aasl/aaslpubsandjournals/slmrb/slmrcontents/volume82005/theory.cfm.

Robert G. Hamlin, S. A. S., *Generic Behavioural Criteria of Managerial Effectiveness,* European Industrial Training, 2008, Vol. 32 No. 4

Strauss, K., Griffin, M. A., & Rafferty, A. E., "Proactivity directed toward the team and the organization: The role of leadership, commitment, and role-breadth self-efficacy", *British Journal of Management.* (in press).

Parker, S. K., Williams, H. M., & Turner, N. (2006). "Modelling the antecedents of proactive behavior at work", *Journal of Applied Psychology*, 91(3), 636-652.

Thompson, Leigh L. (2008) *Making the Team*, 3rd International ed., Pearson Education (US): [distributor] Pearson Education.

Tropham,J.E. (2003). *Making Meetings Work: Achieving High Quality Group Decisions* (2nd 3d). Thousans Oaks, CA:Sage

Use of MDI/SOA Concepts in Industry

Use of MDI/SOA Concepts in Industry

Guy Doumeingts, GFI, France
Martine Grandin-Dubost, GFI, France
gdoumeingts@gfi.fr, mgrandindubost@gfi.fr

Brian Elvesæter, Arne-Jørgen Berre, Einar Landre: Application of SHAPE Technologies in Production and Process Optimization
SINTEF and Statoil

R. Young, N. Chungoora, Z. Usman, N. Anjum, G. Gunendran, C. Palmer, J. Harding, K. Case and A.-F. Cutting-Decelle: An exploration of foundation ontologies and verification methods for manufacturing knowledge sharing
Loughborough University-Wolfson School of Mechanical & Manufacturing Engineering and Laboratoire de Génie Industriel de Lille, Ecole Centrale de Lille

Nabila Zouggar, Mickaël Romain, Guy Doumeingts, Sébastien Cazajous, Yves Ducq, Christophe Merlo, Martine Grandin-Dubost: ISTA3 Methodology
University of Bordeaux - IMS/LAPS, ESTIA, GFI and MIPNET SAS

MDI/SOA Workshop Chairs' Message

The objective of the workshop is to present some examples of use of MDI/SOA (Model-Driven Interoperability/Services-Oriented Architecture) in industry. This workshop was organized in the frame of the Task Force MDI/SOA of INTEROP-VLab. The goal of the Task Force is to elaborate and continuously update a State of the Art in the domain of SOA/MDI, to present methods to implement the concepts, to collect training to disseminate these concepts in industry.

The topics which are analyzed are:

– powerful transformation and mediation language(s) for interoperability mappings;

– support for semantic interoperability for service and process;

– analysis of Semantic proximity;

– use of ontology federation tools;

– effective tools support for user-assisted decisions on matches and mismatches.

This workshop shows the application of MDI combined with SOA and the associated technology (BPM, Enterprise Modeling, ontology, mediation, model transformation, etc.) in industry. The three papers will be based on three projects:

ISTA 3 project: ("Interoperabilité de 3ème génération pour les Sous-Traitants de l'Aéronautique" (Interoperability of 3rd Generation for the sub-contractors in Aeronautics)). In order to be competitive, the sub-contractors must develop flexible and interoperable solutions. The goal of ISTA3 is to develop this type of solution in the domain of the manufacturing of Composite Material parts using the most recent results in Enterprise Modelling, MDI, SOA, Performance Indicators, Ontologies.

This project is supported by the French Ministry of Industry, in the frame of the French Worldwide Aeronautics "Pole de compétitivité Aerospace Valley" in the South West of France (Midi-Pyrénées and Aquitaine regions). SHAPE (Semantically-enabled Heterogenous Service Architecture and Platforms

Engineering) (ICT-2007-216408) (http://www.shape-project.eu/) is a European Research Project under the 7th Framework Program that develops an infrastructure for the model-driven engineering. The paper presents the application of the SHAPE technologies in the Production and Process Optimization industrial use case at Statoil. The Interoperable Manufacturing Knowledge Systems (IMKS) project is a UK research programme funded through the government's Engineering and Physical Sciences Research Council (EPSRC). It is supported by the aerospace and automotive industries, a number of software vendors and undertaken in collaboration with Ecole Centrale de Lille in France. Its aim is to contribute to radically new methods for interoperable manufacturing knowledge sharing that are geared to support dynamic multi-disciplinary engineering design and manufacture, while also contributing to a reference model for manufacturing industry interoperability.

Guy Doumeingts, *GFI, Business Consulting,*
Emeritus Professor, University of Bordeaux 1, France
Martine Grandin-Dubost, *GFI, Business Consulting*

Application of SHAPE Technologies in Production and Process Optimization

Brian Elvesæter* — Arne-Jørgen Berre* — Einar Landre**

*SINTEF ICT
P. O. Box 124 Blindern
N-0314 Oslo
Norway
brian.elvesater@sintef.no
arne.j.berre@sintef.no

** Statoil
Forusbeen 50
N-4035 Stavanger
Norway
einla@statoil.com

ABSTRACT. *SHAPE (ICT-2007-216408) is a European Research Project under the 7th Framework Programme that develops an infrastructure for model-driven engineering for service-oriented landscapes. The technologies are tested, demonstrated and evaluated by two industrial use case partners. This paper presents the application of the SHAPE technologies in the Production and Process Optimization industrial use case at Statoil. Statoil is an integrated technology-based international energy company primarily focused on upstream oil and gas operations.*

KEYWORDS: *model-driven architecture, service-oriented architecture, production and process optimization*

1. Introduction

SHAPE (Semantically-enabled Heterogenous Service Architecture and Platforms Engineering) (ICT-2007-216408) (http://www.shape-project.eu/) is a European Research Project under the 7th Framework Programme that develops an infrastructure for model-driven engineering for service-oriented landscapes with support for various technology platforms and extensions for advanced service provision and consumption techniques.

The technologies developed in the project are centered around SoaML [OMG 2009a], which is a metamodel for describing service-oriented landscapes that is standardized in OMG. SoaML is extended with metamodels for other technology platforms and advanced service engineering techniques. The project provides an integrated tool suite that supports the modeling on the basis of the metamodels, encompasses the necessary model transformations, and a methodology framework that provides role-specific guided procedures for creating all model types and supports the creation of customized methodologies for individual engineering projects.

The technologies are tested, demonstrated, and evaluated by two industrial use case partners. Saarstahl AG, a German steel manufacturer, expects substantial benefits for integrating legacy systems and in particular for the integration of the agent-based production line planning system from applying the SHAPE technologies. Statoil, the largest Norwegian oil and gas company, expects improved practices for business and IT modeling, increased support for flexible event and action management, and more intelligent solutions supporting increased data volumes and improved decision-making support from applying the SHAPE technologies.

This paper focuses on the application of the SHAPE technologies in the Production and Process Optimization (PPO) industrial use case at Statoil. The paper is structured as follows: in section 2 we present the PPO use case and the chosen SHAPE technologies that are applied. Section 3 describes the service-oriented modeling of the use case from a business perspective and section 4 describes the service-oriented modeling from an IT perspective. Finally, section 5 concludes this paper.

2. Production and Process Optimization (PPO) case study

The Norwegian Oil Industry Association (OLF) has defined the term Integrated Operations (IO) as "real time data onshore from offshore fields and new integrated work processes" and has estimated the economic potential of IO to be in the magnitude of 300 billion NOK [OLF 2007]. The technical implication from IO is an increased exchange of information across geographical and organizational boundaries, internally and externally. These requirements drive for new IT solutions, solutions not possible to implement using the more traditional approaches to software development. For this information exchange to be successful, good interoperable IT solutions and standards are needed.

For major actors at the Norwegian Continental Shelf (NCS) such as Statoil the focus now is implementation of IO generation 1 solutions and strategic planning of IO generation 2 solutions. Generation 1 activities focus on integration across onshore and offshore, while generation 2 activities focus on integration across companies. Statoil is an integrated technology-based international energy company primarily focused on upstream oil and gas operations. A joint venture Production and Process Optimization (PPO) project [Sagli, *et al.* 2007] between Statoil and Schlumberger serves as an industrial use case for the SHAPE project.

The use case is concerned with improved reservoir management and production optimization. The aim is to provide an integrated solution for optimizing the reservoir performance, intelligent wells and production processes among the numerous offshore production sites. The processes are currently performed by production experts supported by an IT landscape which consists of various isolated and heterogenous legacy systems of a considerably high complexity that is necessary to provide the required high-quality information.

In order to support the reservoir management process, a prototyping process has been developed for surveillance workflow development and deployment. The dynamic prototyping process allows a bottom-up development of workflows starting from data conditioning and reconciliation up to optimization and control. This should work together with a workflow advisor enabled for improved decision making, streamlining of model updating and other tasks. The workflows depend on a set of software components as shown in Figure 1.

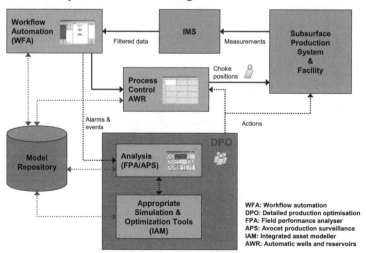

Figure 1. *System components and data flow*

In the SHAPE project we are investigating how to further improve this process by applying service-oriented modeling practices and technologies developed in SHAPE. This is concerned with designing a service-based infrastructure for integrating the information from various subsurface and topside dwelling and production facilities, which are locally distributed and utilize different, often heterogenous information representation and IT systems. The aim is to better align the business processes and optimize the production process, which has great business surplus value for Statoil.

The realization of the PPO scenario faces several challenges:

– The first challenge is to enable an integrated and comprehensive modeling of the business processes for managing the production, which involve various locally distributed actors and expose a considerable complexity.

– The second challenge is the design and modeling of the services for enabling a consistent and automated information exchange among the various IT systems as well as the system architecture on how the services shall interoperate, whereby existing systems shall be integrated and new services shall be developed.

3. Modeling the SOA business perspective of the PPO use case

The business-level SOA modeling for the Statoil PPO use case adopts the SHAPE business modeling methodology which prescribes the use of the Business Motivation Model (BMM) [OMG 2008], Business Process Modeling Notation (BPMN) [OMG 2009b] and SoaML modeling languages. The integrated tool suite contains the modeling tool Modelio Enterprise Edition (http://www.modeliosoft.com/) which has been used to define the business models.

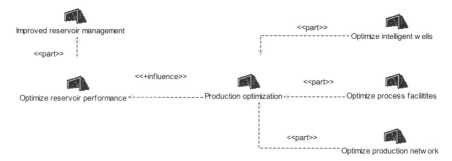

Figure 2. *Business goals (BMM)*

The BMM modeling activity is focused on defining business motivation and the goals of the business operation. Figure 2 shows a goal diagram for the PPO use case, where the two main goals "improved reservoir management" and "production optimization" have been further refined. The business goals can be used to link business processes, roles and services with the business operation.

3.1. *Starting from high-level business processes*

The focus of the use case is the production optimization value chain in the production optimization group (POG). The detailed production optimization (DPO) includes the activities for 1) well surveillance and diagnosis, 2) network optimization, 3) P&I plan draft and 4) identifying intervention candidates. The aim is the harmonization of these sub-processes. This can be done by implementing triggered control elements.

Every supply chain can be further described by process chains using BPMN. Figure 3 shows a detailing of the well surveillance and diagnosis sub-process modeled by business architects at Statoil. On each asset each well shall have one person assigned and responsible for the well surveillance, monitoring and optimization.

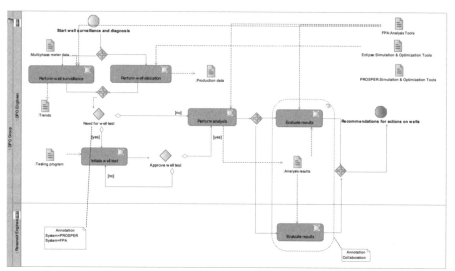

Figure 3. *Well surveillance and diagnosis (BPMN)*

3.2. *Services architecture*

Based on the BPMN process descriptions for each of the four sub-processes. the SHAPE methodology prescribes the specification of a services architecture using SoaML.

A services architecture denotes a business community and focuses on how all the participants in the community work together by providing and using each other's services. Figure 4 shows the high-level services architecture for the production and process optimization at the POG-level as a UML collaboration. Lanes in BPMN represent participants or departments and are modeled as parts (instances of SoaML participants) in the services architecture. Interactions, e.g. passing data between lanes in BPMN, identify potential service usage and are modeled as collaboration uses (instances of SoaML service contracts) in a services architecture.

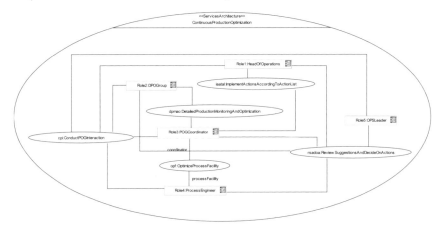

Figure 4. *Services architecture (SoaML)*

3.3. Service contracts

The interaction points of these collaboration uses in the services architecture must be further defined as service contracts for the participants. A service contract is the specification of the agreement between providers and consumers of a service as to what information and obligations will flow between the parties defining the service. Figure 5 shows the initial service contract for the "OptimizeProcessFacility" collaboration use defined in Figure 4.

Figure 5. *Service contract (SoaML)*

4. Modeling the SOA IT perspective of the PPO use case

The IT-level SOA modeling for the Statoil PPO scenario adopts the SHAPE technology platform modeling methodology that prescribes the use of SoaML for defining platform-independent specifications that can be transformed into Web services-based architecture realizations. SHAPE also provides UML extensions to SoaML to support Semantic Web Services (SWS) and Agent technologies.

4.1. Service interfaces

The starting point for the IT-level SOA modeling is the business SOA model that specifies the services architecture and the service contracts.

Figure 6. *Participants, ports, provided and required interfaces (SoaML)*

Figure 6 shows the participants in the services architecture with ports corresponding to the service interfaces (with provided and required interfaces) defined in the initial service contract from Figure 5. These participants correspond to roles from the BPMN process. The service contracts must be further refined with respect to software components that are used by the identified participants to fulfill their service obligations.

The IT-level modeling activity is focused on establishing a service-oriented architecture with well-defined software services to support the business processes. SoaML supports the specification of software services using simple interfaces and service interfaces. The simple interface focuses attention on a one-way interaction provided by a participant on a port represented as a UML interface, whereas the service interface based approach allows for bi-directional services, i.e. supporting callbacks from the provider to the consumer as part of a conversation between the participants.

The diversity of applications at Statoil suggests the usage of standard-based services. In this particular use case we want to investigate the usage of the PRODML standard (http://www.prodml.org/) to implement the identified service interfaces. The PRODML standard defines a set of Web services and corresponding XML schemas. Statoil has identified a suitable Web service from the standard that obtains production volume data as specified by a production volume schema.

Figure 7 below shows the SoaML specification of the PRODML interface for the production volume Web service. The diagram contains an interface with the service operations according to a document-orientated style where message types are passed as arguments and returned as outputs. The structure of the message type is also shown in the figure and is based on the production volume schema. This interface will fulfill the requirements of the ProcessFacility interface identified in the service contract.

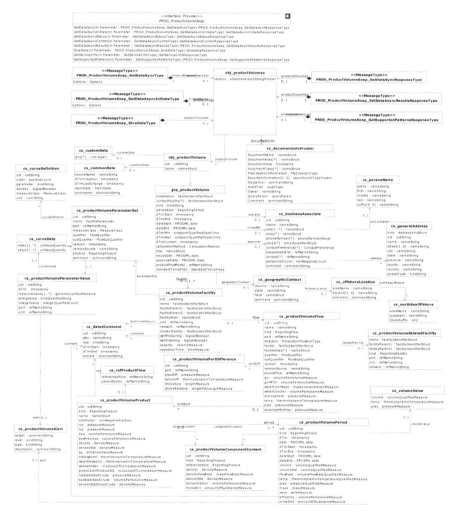

Figure 7. *PRODML interface for the production volume Web service (SoaML)*

4.2. *Components*

The specified service interfaces must be realized by software components. SoaML prescribes that these software components can be specified as participants. For complex systems the modeling of software components may also be associated with separate services architecture and corresponding service contracts. In this example, the components represent software specifications and the models can be used for model transformation and/or code-generation down to underlying implementation technologies.

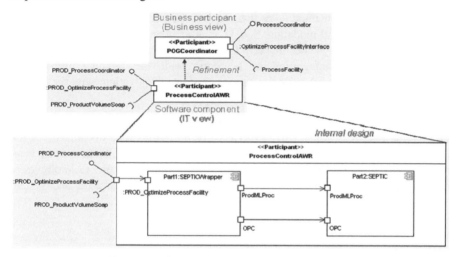

Figure 8. *Software component specification (SoaML)*

Software services in this case could be either a new functionality that must be implemented or wrappers for existing legacy systems. In Figure 8 we see that the ProcessControlAWR software component provides the IT support for the POG Coordinator by realizing the service interface. The ProcessControlAWR component is a composite component that consists of two components. We see that there is an existing application called SEPTIC that offers this functionality through a legacy of interfaces (ProdMLProc and OPC) and that there is a wrapper that provides the PRODML Web service interface (PROD_ProductVolumeSoap).

5. Conclusion

In this paper we have presented an overview of how the SHAPE methodology and in particular the SoaML modeling language has been applied in a top-down manner to model a subset of the Production and Process Optimization (PPO) industrial use case at Statoil. By following the methodology, which uses the SoaML language to represent both a business perspective and an IT perspective of SOA, better business and IT alignment can be achieved since the IT-level model can be viewed as a refinement of the business-level SOA model. Additionally, the SoaML model artefacts can be linked to business goals described in BMM to further help in the alignment process. The SHAPE methodology is currently in the finalization phase and is being revised according to user feedback and experience. Moreover, the methodology is being aligned with the latest changes in the SoaML specification which is also currently under finalization in the OMG.

One aspect of the methodology that requires further work is to provide better guidelines for behavioral modeling. SoaML is quite open with regards to behavioral modeling, and explicitly states that any UML behavior can be used. There is also a synchronization and integration to be done with the ongoing BPMN 2.0 specification, which introduces some service concepts that overlaps with the SoaML specification.

The work presented here has mainly been done in the 7th Framework Programme research project [SHAPE] (ICT-2007-216408). The overall aim of the project is to develop the foundations for the model-driven development of service-oriented system landscapes with support for the integration of other technologies in order to increase the effectiveness and quality of modern software and system engineering.

6. References

[OLF 2007] OLF, "Integrated Operations and the Oil & Gas Ontology", OLF, 2007. http://www.olf.no/getfile.php/zKonvertert/www.olf.no/Rapporter/Dokumenter/070919%20IO%20and%20Ontology%20-%20Brosjyre.pdf

[OMG 2008] OMG, "Business Motivation Model, Version 1.0", Object Management Group, OMG Document formal/2008-08-02, August 2008. http://www.omg.org/spec/BMM/1.0/PDF/

[OMG 2009a] OMG, "Service oriented architecture Modeling Language (SoaML), FTF Beta 1", Object Management Group, OMG Document ptc/2009-04-01, April 2009a. http://www.omg.org/spec/SoaML/1.0/Beta1/PDF/

[OMG 2009b] OMG, "Business Process Model and Notation (BPMN), FTF Beta 1 for Version 2.0", Object Management Group, OMG Document dtc/2009-08-14, August 2009b. http://www.omg.org/spec/BPMN/2.0/Beta1/PDF/

[Sagli, et al. 2007] J. R. Sagli, H. E. Klumpen, G. Nunez, and F. Nielsen, "Improved Production and Process Optimization Through People, Technology, and Process", in *Proc. of the SPE Annual Technical Conference and Exhibition*, Anaheim, California, USA, 2007, Society of Petroleum Engineers. http://www.spe.org/elibrary/servlet/spepreview?id=SPE-110655-MS&speCommonAppContext=ELIBRARY

An Exploration of Foundation Ontologies and Verification Methods for Manufacturing Knowledge Sharing

R. Young* — N. Chungoora* — Z. Usman — N. Anjum* —
G. Gunendran* — C. Palmer* — J.A. Harding* — K. Case* —
A.-F. Cutting-Decelle**

Loughborough University
Wolfson School of Mechanical & Manufacturing Engineering
Loughborough
Leicestershire
UK

**Laboratoire de Génie Industriel de Lille*
Ecole Centrale de Lille
r.i.young@lboro.ac.uk

ABSTRACT. *This paper presents the current status of the Interoperable Manufacturing Knowledge Systems (IMKS) research project. It sets the work into the context of Model Driven Architectures, explores the value of a manufacturing foundation ontology in the context of the design and manufacture of machined components and illustrates potential routes to knowledge verification across domains. It argues for a foundation ontology combined with specialized domain ontologies as well as verification methods combined with query mechanisms. It goes on to illustrate how the level of effective knowledge sharing can be assessed across multiple product design and manufacturing domains.*

KEYWORDS: *MDA, ontology, foundation concepts, verification, interoperability, knowledge sharing*

1. Introduction

Manufacturing companies are starting to tap the benefits of highly sophisticated Information and Communications Technology (ICT) systems such as Product Lifecycle Management (PLM) as a major investment towards maintaining competitive advantage and as a route to managing the increasing complexity of their products and product service systems. However the tightly focused methods currently required in the configuration of such systems do not fit well with requirements for interoperable collaborative engineering. Also, while such systems provide methods for information organization and management, they have significant limitations in terms of representing and sharing manufacturing knowledge, which is a major requirement if future systems are to be able to support the new product introduction process flexibly and effectively. This requires knowledge representation methods that can support the needs of individual skill groups while supporting the need for knowledge sharing across skill groups.

It is clear from the wide range of work in interoperability, highlighted effectively through the work at NIST (Ray and Jones, 2003) and from the investigations of INTEROP that traditional approaches to integrated information sharing fall far short of meeting the requirements for the seamless sharing of information and knowledge to support enterprise activities. Further, work into the use of Model Driven Architectures and Model Driven Interoperability show promise as a route to the understanding and provision of interoperable solutions (Bourey *et al.*, 2006).

The provision of formal semantic definitions through the use of heavyweight ontologies such as the Process Specification language (PSL) (ISO 18629, 2004) and the concept behind the use of heavyweight foundation ontologies has also provided a significant impetus for the work being undertaken in the IMKS project. Our early investigation into the development of an interoperable framework for manufacturing knowledge-sharing based on manufacturing foundation concepts and using PSL, is showing promise (Chungoora and Young, 2010).

The main research question addressed in IMKS is how to develop flexible systems that can share manufacturing knowledge across the domains of product design and manufacturing planning. In particular the work aims to identify a manufacturing foundation ontology and the set of verification methods needed should to support querying across multiple manufacturing domain ontologies.

The research methodology being employed is to determine through industrial investigation the key concepts and verification methods which need to be specified to meet the needs of specific industrial scenarios. System designs are being developed using Common Logic and implemented in an experimental environment in order to test the ideas being developed. The experimental environment is based on the use of the IODE ontology development environment and XKS knowledge base from Highfleet Inc along with Siemens' PLM software as a source and repository for relevant product and manufacturing facility information.

2. The IMKS concept in the context of model driven architectures and international standards

The development of knowledge-sharing systems needs to be considered from the perspective of the methods employed in the specification of the system. Here we see the Model Driven Architecture (MDA) approach as being important to successful systems development.

MDA defines an approach to IT system specification that separates the specification of system functionalities from the specification of the implementation of this functionality on a specific technology platform. The MDA approach should enable the same model functionality to be achieved on multiple platforms through auxiliary mapping standards, or through point mappings to specific platforms.

The architecture defines a hierarchy of models from three different points of view: the Computation Independent Model (CIM), the Platform Independent Model (PIM), and the Platform Specific Model (PSM). The computation independent viewpoint focuses on the environment and the requirements of the system; the details of the structure are hidden or not yet defined. The platform independent viewpoint focuses on the operation of a system while hiding the details necessary to a particular platform. A platform-independent view shows the part of the complete specification that does not change from one platform to another. The platform specific viewpoint combines the platform independent viewpoint with an additional focus on the detail of the use of a specific platform by a system.

For MDA to be effective, model transformations are needed which define the process by which a model is converted to another model of the same system. For example, a transformation tool takes a CIM and transforms it into a PIM. A further transformation tool transforms the PIM into PSM. The transformation tool takes one model as input and produces a second model as output. Generally speaking, a transformation definition consists of a collection of transformation rules, which are unambiguous specifications of the way a part of one model can be used to create a part of another model. However, while this approach provides a very useful approach to systems development it does not, by itself, support interoperability across systems.

When we consider approaches to information sharing, the work of the International Standards Organization's technical committee responsible for industrial automation and integration (ISO TC184/SC4) has been generating standards to support information sharing and exchange for over two decades. Of these, possibly the Standards for Product Data Representation and Exchange (ISO

10303, 1994) has the highest profile as a route to sharing information across CAD systems and PLM systems.

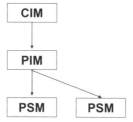

Figure 1. *ISO 10303 standards development in the context of MDA*

If we consider the ISO 10303 approach in the context of MDA then this can be represented as illustrated in Figure 1, where two systems have their own platform-specific model but share the same platform-independent model, i.e. the standard model produced by the ISO. This works well where a single PIM can be used but problems start to arise where multiple PIMs or, in the case of standards such as ISO 10303, multiple Application Protocols are developed.

ISO TC184/SC4 works hard to try to ensure compatibility across its standards but many of the concepts used across these standards rely on textual definitions of the terms being used. This leads to potential problems in a different interpretation of terminology and of inadvertent specializations of terms. For example if we take the concept "product" from ISO 10303-1 this is described as "a thing or substance produced by a natural or artificial process" which both ISO 10303-239 and ISO 10303-41 purport to use. However, when the EXPRESS representation for products is studied it can be seen to be quite different in the two respective standards. So when the same term is apparently used, it is important that there is a mechanism to check whether it really is the same meaning that is used. Similarly if we consider information standards more broadly and consider the set of definitions listed below for the term "process" (Michel 2005), it is interesting to note that when comparing these definitions it is difficult with some of the definitions to tell whether they have the same meaning or not.

PROCESS (ISO/CEN 19439) "partially ordered set of activities that can be executed to achieve some desired end-result in pursuit of a given object".

PROCESS (ISO 15531-1; ISO 18629-1) "structured set of activities involving various enterprise entities, that is designed and organized for a given purpose".

PROCESS (ISO 10303-49) "a particular procedure for doing something involving one or more steps or operations. The process may produce a product, a property a product, or an aspect of a product".

From this we can identify two key issues: (a) How can we ensure the common use of terms when that is the intention? (b) How can we enable specialization of terms but at the same time be able to assess the shareability across two alternative specializations?

We argue that where multiple Platform Independent Models are needed there is a need for a heavy weight ontology which underlies these models to provide a formal set of concepts which can be utilized across the full range of models required. In addition, where concepts are specialized to suit specific domains, there is a need to evaluate the differences in concepts across domains in order to verify the extent to which knowledge across these domain concepts is sharable. This basic idea is illustrated in the context of MDA in Figure 2.

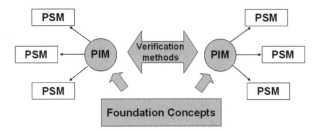

Figure 2. *Sharing across multiple Platform-Independent Models*

Within the IMKS project, our particular interest is in the design and manufacture of machined aerospace and automotive parts and how manufacturing knowledge can be shared across these two domains. Taking this scope and applying it to the concept illustrated in Figure 2 we are therefore investigating the set of foundation concepts applicable to manufacturing facilities and manufactured products, investigating the specialization of these concepts to suit product design and manufacturing planning and investigating how knowledge, based on these specialized concepts can be verified as to its shareability.

The IMKS approach explores the common concepts, defined in a manufacturing foundation ontology and specializes these as necessary to suit product design requirements and also, separately to suit manufacturing engineering requirements. These ontologies can then be used to develop manufacturing knowledge bases to suit design engineers and manufacturing planners respectively. The relationship between the knowledge captured in the two specialized knowledge bases can be assessed via a set of verification methods which are aware of the underlying ontologies on which the knowledge bases are built.

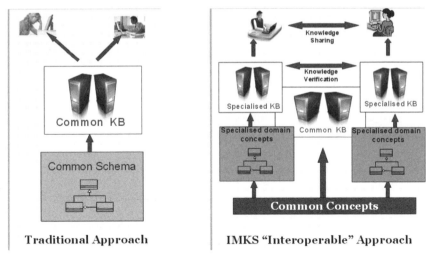

| Traditional Approach | IMKS "Interoperable" Approach |

Figure 3. *The IMKS approach to Interoperability*

It should be noted that these specialized knowledge bases are seen as extensions to shared common knowledge bases. Where common knowledge bases can be used, they negate the need for verification methods to be employed. These ideas are illustrated simply in Figure 3, which compares this approach with the traditional approaches of providing a common knowledge base as the route sharing.

It should also be noted that the type of knowledge we aim to capture is what is sometimes termed best practice knowledge i.e. knowledge where a company has a clear view on how a particular task is best performed. We are not attempting to deal with complex knowledge or attempting to replace key human experts with knowledge bases. We are trying to make knowledge that is well understood by particular expert groups available to other groups where that knowledge is not clearly understood. Across product design and manufacturing planning this is typically seen as an issue of viewpoints, where the designer takes a functional view of the product and the planner takes a manufacturing view of the product.

3. Developing a manufacturing foundation ontology

In this work we are interested in the representation of the common concepts which are used across all domains which have an interest in manufacturing knowledge, but we are particularly focused on knowledge which will be used during product design and manufacturing planning. We have also constrained our manufacturing process interests to machining, only in order to have a manageable scale of problem to investigate.

We have, in previous research (Young *et al.*, 2007), argued the need for a manufacturing foundation ontology and demonstrated how tools like the Process Specification Language can provide a valuable basis for the modeling of manufacturing process concepts. We have also argued for the need to capture knowledge that links manufacturing facilities with the parts which these facilities produce. Hence while some concepts may be generic manufacturing concepts, others will be specific to particular worlds of manufacture e.g. while the machining of automotive parts and aerospace parts have some things in common, there are many aspects of their part manufacture which are radically different. Simplistic examples of the sorts of concepts which need to be included in the foundation ontology and linked to particular worlds of manufacture are provided in Figure 4.

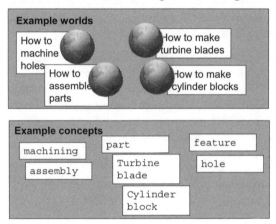

Figure 4. *Some basic concepts and worlds of manufacturing knowledge*

One of key areas where manufacturing knowledge needs to be shared is in product design, as a critical part of product design is to ensure that designs are as easily manufacturable as possible. However, concepts from a design perspective will not be the same as concepts from a manufacturing perspective. For example, when a designer is focused on a feature of a part, he is primarily interested in the functions which that feature provides, while the manufacturing engineer is interested in features from a manufacturing perspective. In some cases, the two perspectives may share common geometry, but in some cases even this may be different.

4. Cross-domain verification methods

When formalized knowledge is shared between different domains, prevention of its subjective interpretation becomes necessary. This process of authentication of the interpretation, here, is referred to as knowledge verification. As used in the IMKS project, knowledge verification can be redefined as the process of ensuring that during the cross domain knowledge sharing, what a certain knowledge entity describes in one domain is correctly understood in the other. An important point to note here is that the definition and steps for the verification of knowledge are a combination of the verification of knowledge-based systems architectures and the verification of knowledge contained within the knowledge bases.

The context of a knowledge entity is crucial in the transfer of semantics across disciplines and an ambiguous context may hinder interoperability. The identification and fixation of context can be done through ontological commitment. Another way of doing this is to map the similar terms in two ontologies belonging to different domains. The similarity finding stage, however, is not straight forward especially when ontologies from different domains are mapped. This is because there can be differences in the use of concepts across different domains.

In the IMKS scenario, two chosen domains are design and manufacturing. Experience from industry shows that different terminologies are used in design and manufacturing domains to refer to the same thing. Examples of these are shown in Figure 5. Due to this problem, if a designer wants to access some knowledge about manufacturing methods, the knowledge system might not be able to find a match on the manufacturing side unless these terms are mapped.

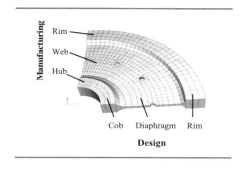

Figure 5. *Examples of the use of alternative terms*

5. A framework for manufacturing knowledge sharing

Our initial investigation of the IMKS concept focused on the targeted domain of holes: holes from a design perspective, e.g. a bolt hole, and holes from a manufacturing perspective, e.g. a counterbore hole. The research (Chungoora, 2010) led to the proposal of a framework for semantic interoperability consisting of four layers as illustrated in Figure 6. The bottom two layers provide the foundation concepts and the specialization mechanisms of these concepts into domains. In our case the particular domains are design and manufacture. The upper two layers provide methods of reconciling the meaning across sets of domain concepts and applying these methods to evaluate the level of sharing which can be achieved across two specific domains.

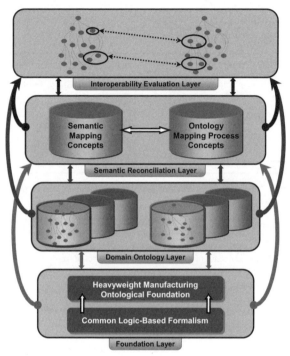

Figure 6. *A framework for manufacturing interoperability*

6. Initial cross domain knowledge sharing experiments

An experimental system has been implemented in Common Logic with the foundation layer using elements of PSL and extending elements of ISO 10303-224 and other existing product representations. This has then been used to produce specialized concepts for design domains and manufacturing domains, as well as to support the development of mapping and merging concepts in the semantic reconciliation layer. A set of queries have also been defined in the interoperability evaluation layer.

A number of experiments have been undertaken to explore the various aspects of the framework. Here we describe one such experiment which takes models of two parts which have been defined using two different domain ontologies, that have been based on the same foundation ontology. Portions of these parts are illustrated in

Figure 7 which also highlights the two hole features which are to be compared in the analysis.

The instances are queried in order to check their semantic compatibility which results in a list of mapping relations describing the correspondences and differences between the features. Examples of these are illustrated in Figure 8.

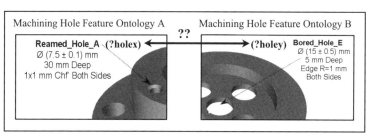

Figure 7. *Instances of holes to be compared across two ontologies*

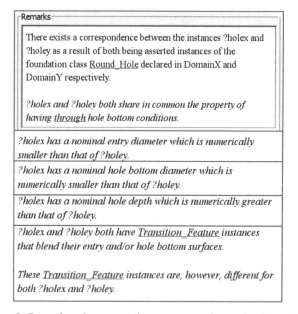

Figure 8. *Examples of cross-ontology correspondences for the two holes*

7. Conclusions

We have argued that a manufacturing foundation ontology, combined with a set of verification methods, has the potential to support improved interoperability across domains which need to share manufacturing knowledge. We have illustrated how this supports the concepts of model-driven interoperability and can contribute, in principle, to improved methods for information-sharing standards development.

We have shown, through an initial experimental framework how these ideas can be combined to assess the correspondences that exist between two heterogenous knowledge bases in order to evaluate their level of interoperability. We are currently exploring the application of these ideas to industrially relevant scenarios.

This work is of fundamental importance to industry as it has the potential to radically improve the design for manufacture activity and hence improve the drive towards robust design and the general all pervasive industrial need for "better, faster, cheaper". From an academic perspective, the work has already led to two complementary projects; one exploring methods for sharing manufacturing knowledge through the full product lifecycle and one exploring methods by which knowledge held in knowledge bases should be maintained and kept up-to-date.

8. Acknowledgements

This research is funded by EPSRC through the Innovative Manufacturing and Construction Research Centre in Loughborough University (IMCRC project 253).

9. References

Almeida J.P., Dijkman R., Sinderen M.V., Pires L.S., (2005), "Platform-independent modelling in MDA: supporting abstract platforms", in: *Model Driven Architecture: European MDA Workshop*, MDAFA, June 10-11, 2004, Linkping, Sweden.

Bourey J.P., Grangel R., Doumeingts G. and Berre A., 2006. INTEROP NoE: Deliverable DTG2.2: Report on Model Interoperability.

Chungoora N., (2010) A Framework to Support Semantic Interoperability in Product Design and Manufacture, PhD thesis, Loughborough University, Loughborough, UK.

Chungoora N., Young R.I.M., (2010), "A framework to support semantic interoperability in product design and manufacture", accepted for publication in 20th CIRP Design Conference, Nantes, France.

ISO 10303-1, (1994). Industrial Automation Systems and Integration – Product Data Representation and Exchange – Part 1: Overview and Fundamental Principles.

ISO 10303-224.3, (2003) Product data representation and exchange: Application protocol: Mechanical product definition for process planning using machining features.

ISO 18629-1, ISO TC184/SC4/JWG8, Industrial Automation System and Integration – Process Specification Language: Part 1. Overview and Basic Principles, 2004.

ISO/IEC-24707, 2007, International Standard, First edition 2007-10-01 Information technology – Common Logic (CL): a framework for a family of logic based languages

ISO TC184/SC4 http://www.tc184-sc4.org

Michel J.J, Terminology extracted from some manufacturing and related standards, *Proposal for New Standardization Work* CEN/TC 310 N1119R3, 2005.

Ray S.R., Jones A.T., (2003) Manufacturing interoperability. "Concurrent Engineering, Enhanced Interoperable Systems", *Proceedings of the 10th ISPE International Conference*, Madeira Island, Portugal: 535–540

Young R.I.M, Gunendran A.G, Cutting-Decelle A.F., Gruninger M, (2007), "Manufacturing knowledge sharing in PLM: a progression towards the use of heavy weight ontologies", *International Journal of Production Research*, Vol. 45, No. 7, 1 April, 1505–1519

ISTA3 Methodology Application Case

Nabila Zouggar* — Mickaël Romain** — Guy Doumeingts*** — Sébastien Cazajous**** — Yves Ducq* — Christophe Merlo** — Martine Grandin-Dubost***

* University of Bordeaux - IMS/LAPS
351 cours de la libération, 33405 Talence cedex
nabila.zouggar@ims-bordeaux.fr
yves.ducq@ims-bordeaux.fr

** ESTIA
Technopole Izarbel, 64210 Bidart
m.romain@estia.fr
c.merlo@estia.fr

*** GFI
15 rue Beaujon, 75008 Paris
gdoumeingts@gfi.fr
mgrandi-dubost@gfi.fr

**** MIPNET SAS
53 route d'Espagne, 31000 Toulouse
tito@mipnet.info

ABSTRACT. *The aeronautical sector is one of the most versatile in which reorganizations are mandatory to survive. The strategy of the main aircraft manufacturers is to sub-contract more and more the design and manufacturing of the aircraft parts or set of parts. In such a context, the sub-contractors develop complex relationships with the principals. These relationships are implemented through various IT services which must be interoperable in order that the enterprises keep their competitiveness. The goal of this paper is to present the methodology to develop Interoperability Services Utilities (ISU) for aircraft sub-contractors. This methodology is developed in the frame of ISTA3 project. The first part presents the ISTA 3 project, the second describes the methodology developed, the third presents the first results of the project and the last one will introduce the future works.*

KEYWORDS: *model-driven interoperability, GRAI methodology, aeronautics sub-contractors, enterprise modeling, business process modeling, model transformation*

1. Introduction

This paper presents the ISTA3 project (**I**nteropérabilité de **3**^{ème} génération pour les **S**ous-**T**raitants de l'**A**éronautique – Interoperability of 3rd generation (I3rdG) for the Aeronautics Sub-contractors), more specifically the methodology to design, develop and implement ISUs (Interoperability Services Utilities: services solutions adaptable and reusable) for I3rdG. This project is funded by the French Ministry of Industry and supported by the "Pole de Compétitivité" Aerospace Valley located in both Regions Midi-Pyrénées (Toulouse) and Aquitaine (Bordeaux). One of the objectives of the project is to demonstrate the interest of IESA (Interoperability for Enterprise Systems and Applications) for Industry.

This research work starts from the results of INTEROP-NoE (Interoperability Research for Networked Enterprise Applications and Software, a Network of Excellence supported by European Commission 2004-2007, FP6 508011, 42 months, 50 partners, 6,5 M€ EC funds), especially some results of TG2 (Task Group N°2). In this TG2, the concepts of MDI (Model-Driven Interoperability) were developed [Bourey *et al.*, 2007].

The main originality of ISTA3 project is developing a complete methodology and the associated IT applications based on MDI, supported by Enterprise Modeling Techniques, using SOA (Services Oriented Architectures), combined with Ontology to develop ISUs for I3rdG. The organization of this paper is the following: the first part presents the ISTA 3 project, the second describes the status of the developed methodology, the third presents the first application of the methodology to the project and the last part introduces future works.

2. Presentation of ISTA 3 project

The strategy of the main aeronautics manufacturers is to sub-contract more and more the design and manufacturing of parts or sets of parts. For example, AIRBUS has the objective to decrease the internal volume of manufacturing from 60% to 30%, following the evolution of the automotive industry.

Today the trend is to develop a "risk partnership": the aeronautics manufacturers supply the initial technical specifications and refine them by an iterative work with the sub-contractors.

In such a context, the sub-contractors develop complex relationships with the principals and the other sub-contractors. These relationships concern all the problems of the Supply Chain and the connected functions: purchasing, order processing, exchange of documentation, project follow up, etc. The solutions are implemented through various IT applications such as CAD (Computer Aided Design), PDM (Products Data Management) or PLM (Product Lifecycle

Management), ERP (Enterprise Resources Planning) etc, but also IT services. In order to be competitive and reactive, the sub-contractors must use Interoperable IT solutions. This interaction with the partners must be performed at a lower cost, taking in account the existing investments and anticipating the next technological evolutions.

The IESA domain is becoming a major challenge for the sub-contractors in the aeronautics industry: 40% of the enterprise IT costs is the consequence of the non-interoperability of IT applications (source: the Yankee Group 2001).

ISTA3 is a finalized project: the results are methodology and prototypes which will be implemented and tested in real situations brought by the industrial partners of the projects which are SMEs.

The industrial case is formed by one sub-contractor in composite material of rank 2 (called in this paper SC 1) and two sub-contractors in composite material of rank 3 (called in this paper SC 2 and SC 3) (see Figure 1).

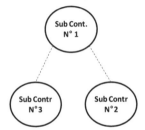

Figure 1. *ISTA3 industrial case*

The project develops I3rdG solutions and also compares the results with an Interoperability of 2nd generation (I2nd G).

We recall that INTEROP NoE has defined interoperability as the ability of an Enterprise to interact with other Enterprises not only on an Information Technology point of view but also on organizational and semantic point of views. This interaction must be flexible and developed at the lower cost. In the context of networked enterprises, interoperability refers to the ability of interactions (exchange of information and services) between enterprise systems. Interoperability is considered as significant if the interactions can take place on four different levels: Data, Services, Processes and Systems, with a semantics defined in a given business context [Chen, 2006].

Incompatibility (due to the heterogeneity) between the systems is the main cause of non-interoperability. There are several approaches to suppress the non-interoperability [Chen *et al.*, 2003]. We will take into consideration the interoperability barriers. To suppress these interoperability barriers there are three types of solutions:

(a) the first generation (integrated approach) uses a standard format to exchange the information;

(b) the second generation (unified approach) uses a metamodel of the standard to exchange the information;

(c) the third generation (federated approach) uses the ontology in order to adapt dynamically the exchange of information. This last approach brings more flexibility.

ISTA 3 contributes to the test of the 2nd generation: there is a French project **SEINE** (Standards pour l'Entreprise Innovante Numérique Etendue) developed by AFNET (French Association of INTERNET development "Association Francophone pour le development d'internet") which has developed a platform in order to transfer product design information from SC1 using the STEP[1] standard (see Figure 2). Using this platform, the product data are transformed from the standard of SC1 to the standard of SC2 or SC3 using specific connectors. So, the problem is that for each kind of collaboration, new connectors must be developed which cannot be re-used for other transformations. Then the information stored on the platform in STEP format is transferred to the SC2 using a second connector.

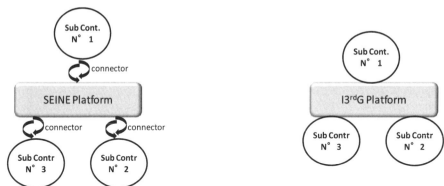

Figure 2. *SEINE platform*   **Figure 3.** *I3ʳᵈG platform*

In the $I3^{rd}G$ approach, the information between the SCs is exchanged through a platform (Figure 3) developed with the SOA principles. The project produces a set of ISUs more generic than the connectors reusable and adaptable according to the evolution of IT systems of the sub-contractors.

---

1 In design and manufacturing, many systems are used to manage technical product data. Each system has its own data formats. The most known standard supported by ISO is STEP (Standard for Product Model Data).

Moreover, in order to disseminate and implement the results efficiently, ISTA3 develops a complete vocational course which accompanies the project in order to disseminate the produced know-how. This course will be available through the e-learning platform of INTEROP-VLab.[2]

ISTA 3 analyzes the possibility of transferring the results of I3rdG solutions to other domains such as wiring in the aeronautics industry.

3. Presentation of the methodology to develop ISTA3 solutions

Based on the objectives of the project and the requirements given by the sub-contractors in their relationships, we underline that we have to answer the following requirements:

– to cooperate with the principals and the sub-contractors along the life cycle of the products;

– to evaluate continuously the performance a priori in order to anticipate on the results and *a posteriori* to check the evolution of the performances and to evaluate the risks;

– to use the enterprise modeling techniques in order to satisfy the requirements of the MDI architecture starting at business level and to maintain a continuum and coherence at all levels of the architecture.

One originality of the approach is to start at the Business level. We estimate that often the majority of projects don't take into account the constraints issued from this level.

The proposed methodology is composed of five phases:

– a preliminary phase to evaluate the potentiality of the collaborations between the sub-contractors;

– a modeling phase at the CIM level in order to determine the requirements;

– a design and development phase at the PIM and PSM level to produce the solutions using SOA techniques and Enterprise Service Bus to orchestrate the services;

– an implementation phase of the solutions inside the sub-contractors;

– an evaluation phase a posteriori in order to check if the initial objectives are reached and to maintain a continuous check.

We underline that in such a project, the implementation of the methodology is not linear. Part of the research will be dedicated to evaluating the possibility of

---

2 www.interop-vlab.eu.

combining a top-down approach with a bottom-up approach: the transformation must be reversible.

3.1. *Phase 1*

The aim of this phase is to evaluate the potentiality of cooperation of sub-contractors. This is performed through a bearing questionnaire on the knowledge of its cooperation capacity with partners. This is a short phase (no more than one day) which allows us to quickly determine the potentiality of the sub-contractors to cooperate with others and then to minimize risks for the principals [Doumeingts *et al.*, 1993].

This questionnaire is divided into four categories: general enterprise information, design department, industrialization department and logistics department including planning, sourcing, production and distribution.

The questionnaire aims to evaluate seven main interoperability indicators:

– Complexity, diversity of exchange: how many cooperations, frequency of modifications in exchanges, volume of exchanges by cooperation.

– Interoperability of Information System (technical interoperability).

– Interoperability of practices (organizational interoperability).

– Semantic interoperability (terminologies, standards, re-works due to understanding problems, ontologies, internal glossary).

– Maturity: which knowledge of the system, what master of the system, which master of the control and of the evolution management (in terms of skills).

– Type of interoperability – type of cooperation (integrated, unified, federated) for each function – in which way do they solve interoperability problems.

– Risks of not evolving, risks of changing to become interoperable.

The result enables us to have information on the way in which the enterprise works with its partners but also the organization of its information system.

3.2. *Phase 2*

Concerning the CIM level, which consists of modeling the sub-contractors at the business level, it is decomposed into two sub-phases (see Figure 4):

– The top CIM in which first the AS IS of each sub-contractor is built: this could be the complete enterprise (in case of SMEs) or a part of the enterprise, the parts which are in cooperation. From these two AS IS we deduce one common TO BE focusing on the cooperation between the two enterprises. For this task we use GRAI modeling [Doumeingts *et al.*, 1993, 1998, 2001].

– The bottom CIM which focuses on the modeling of the previous cooperation system part which will be computerized. This is a sub-system of the Top CIM common model: we use also GRAI modeling in order to deduce the model from TOP CIM and to check the coherence. Then this model is transformed by model transformation with specific tools orientated towards business process modeling.

This phase is coherent: it concerns the elaboration of the specifications of the solutions. The use of Enterprise Modeling Techniques (EMT) facilitates, at the CIM level, the representation and thus the understanding and the optimization of the relationships between sub-contractors from the strategic level to the tactical level and the operational level. The model transformation is used to go from the top CIM level to the bottom CIM level. There is ongoing research on this point.

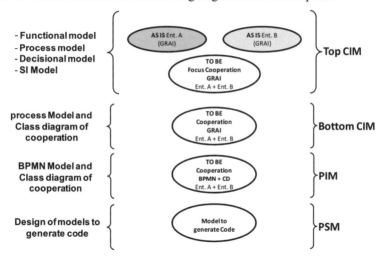

Figure 4. *The MDI architecture for ISTA 3*

The GRAI methodology recommends representing the structure and the running of the enterprises and of their collaboration through several models: the functional view which gives global view of the enterprise, the physical process system which describes the operational part of the enterprise, the decisional system which controls the physical process, the information system. BPMN was chosen because this is the technique to represent business processes at a detailed level, using the results of top CIM models and which facilitate the transition towards the simulation and computerization of processes. The methodology to build the models will be described in the next section: the phases AS IS and TO BE and also the principles to collect the information.

3.3. *Phase 3*

The transformation from CIM to PIM then from PIM to PSM which allows building the USIs based on the SOA approach. The identification and the development of services based on top and bottom CIM models are the basis of the logical architecture to enable interoperability. In fact, several kinds of services are developed: business services and technical services. Business services are extracted from the model thanks to the transformations. The technical services are basic services which are composed to build business services.

Ontology is exploited to provide the necessary support to a federated approach of interoperability. This ontology should lead to the emergence of a semantic and taxonomic common framework to the partners; ease the shared information exchanges and the data processing, as well as the evolution of the information system. Two ontologies are in development: one generic ontology for the concerned domain (design and manufacturing of composite material products) and particular ontologies for each industrial case.

SOA provides concepts and technologies based on the concept of services whose benefit is the ease of connection / disconnection of new "partners" (applications) and the adaptability of the interface to take into account the new operational needs. Resulting methodology will provide a service oriented architecture framework, to systematize the transformation of business process models in to services (ISU).

3.4. *Phase 4*

The implementation of solutions: in this phase, the technical and business services are implemented and an Enterprise Service Bus is implemented to support service orchestration. The method used is based on the re-using of the TO BE Top CIM and TO BE Bottom CIM models. These models will support:

– the training of the future users;
– the creation of an adapted documentation for the users;
– the adaptation of the users to the change;
– the evaluation of the performance of the implemented solution.

3.5. *Phase 5*

Performance evaluation: performance indicators will be implemented in order to evaluate the interoperability degree. In fact, the enterprise activities will be decomposed in an activity of interoperability alignment and a business activity. The interoperability performance will be measured on the first activity and the generic performance indicators (as service level, cost, lead time, etc.) will be measured on the second part of the activity. The definition of the Performance indicators will be supported by the TO BE Top CIM model. Methods as ECOGRAI or simulations will be used to define performance indicators and to evaluate their value *a priori* before the implementation of ISUs.

4. Case study

We will describe the Case Study for phase 1, 2 and 3 for the relationship between subcontractor 1 and subcontractor 2

4.1. *Phase 1: result for sub-contractor 1*

The results of the questionnaire assessing sub-contractor 1, has shown that it is in cooperation with four principals and four suppliers. We can conclude after combining the responses of sub-contractor 1 with interoperability indicators defined above that this sub-contractor is consistent with the development on the I3rdG. This evaluation will be extended to the other sub-contractors.

4.2. *Phase 2: CIM level*

This level is decomposed into two steps. The first covers the top CIM and second the bottom CIM.

4.2.1. *Top CIM*

The objective is to model the sub-contractors (SC1 and SC2) in the parts where the interoperability will be developed. The GRAI method enabled us to build different models from the functional, physical, decisional, informational points of view. Top CIM phase is divided into two parts.

4.2.1.1. AS- IS Top CIM

This sub-phase of modeling is devoted to recovering information concerning the current state of the cooperation from the point of view of each sub-contractor. Then we obtain a model for each company including the cooperation. Only parts of the company implied in cooperation are modeled. The models obtained are used to analyze the actual situation of cooperation and to define the strong points and the points that could be improved.

A very important aspect of the GRAI methodology is the process of collecting the information with the definition of the participants, the organization of the various meetings. This process to collect the information defines a serial of meetings with the main deciders (Synthesis Group (SG)) combined with interviews "on the floor" of key actors.

The GRAI specialist advises and support the SG. This process to collect the information allows us to produce the following results:

– the functional view: this is a general view, we identify the main functions of the subcontractor (Customer Relationship, Support, Production, etc.) as well as the main relationships between them;

– the Physical Processes System which describes the main processes with "added value", which contribute directly, deliver the products or the services to the customer; the "trade" view of the company;

– the decisional grid allows to define the main decisions at the various levels: tactical, strategic and operational in order to control the Physical Processes System in order to reach the assigned objectives;

– an aggregated Information model using Class Diagram is also produced with the description of the main associated data;

The result of this phase is the AS IS top CIM model of each sub contractor oriented towards the cooperation between them.

4.2.1.2. TO BE Top CIM

This sub-phase implies the two subcontractors. The model at the TO BE Top CIM is built based on the results of the modeling at the Top CIM AS-IS. This model which is unique contains the processes and the information defining the cooperation between the two sub contractors (see Figure 5). The model GRAI TO BE TOP CIM describes mainly the cooperation based on the physical processes and also the decisional processes (we notice the importance of the decisions in the cooperation between two sub-contractors). A more detailed information system is also produced. To create these models, we use a Synthesis Group with concerned representatives of the two partners.

This TO BE Top CIM model allows us to clearly identify the various points of interoperability between the partners and to describe them in detail. Some rules have been defined to facilitate the modeling and to guide the search for the optimized model. To build the GRAI Models we used GraiTools distributed and maintained by GFI.

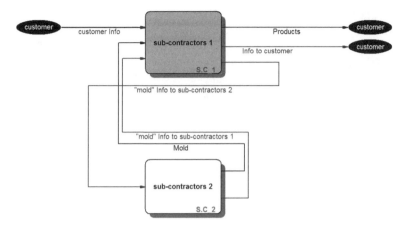

Figure 5. *TO BE TOP CIM*

4.2.2. *TO BE Bottom CIM of cooperation*

TO BE *Bottom* CIM model is an extraction of TO BE Top CIM model. This model focuses essentially on the computerized part of the cooperation between the two sub-contractors (see Figure 6). This model describes directly the processes (physical and decisional) identified in the cooperation at the TO BE Top CIM level.

The model of the Information System is elaborate based on the Information model at the TO BE Top CIM model. The level of detail is increased.

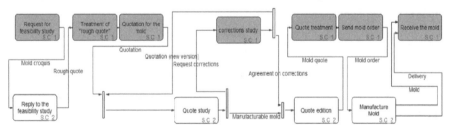

Figure 6. *TO BE Bottom CIM using GRAI*

The research is orientated toward the semi-automatic transformation from the TO BE top CIM toward the TO BE Bottom CIM.

The TO BE bottom CIM model is composed of:

– process model of cooperation in which we indicate sub-contractor 1 (in gray), sub-contractor 2 (in white) and the exchange of information;

– the associated Information System model with additional details (example of documents used currently).

We notice that the project is not finished and there is still discussion on the location of the transformation from GRAI model to BPMN model at the TO BE Bottom CIM. We recommend performing a first transformation from TO BE top CIM to TO BE bottom CIM with the same modeling technique (GRAI) in order to check the coherence then to transform the TO BE bottom CIM from GRAI to BPMN. This transformation could be done at the bottom CIM or from bottom CIM to PIM. In this case we have chosen to perform this transformation in the second case.

4.3. *Phase 3: Transformation from CIM to PIM to PSM*

The TO BE bottom CIM is described with the GRAI models mainly the physical and decisional processes and the class diagram.

The transformation to the PIM level consists of transforming the GRAI processes in BPMN (the class diagrams will be refined). This transformation has been developed by [Lemrabet *et al.*, 2010], [Grangel *et al.*, 2009]. It consists mainly:

– of transforming the source model (GRAI Extended Actigram) in the target model (processes of BPMN);

– of defining the mapping by analyzing the source metamodel and the target metamodel in order to build the meta-meta model of the transformation.

The conditions to perform the transformation are the following:

– to have a deep knowledge on the meta model of the source and the target in order to define the mapping;

– a language to code the mapping model and a tool to execute it;

– a tool to create the sources model compatible with the transformation tool;

– a graphical tool to visualize the target models.

In ISTA 3 (and also in another project ASICOM which develops interoperability in the domain of Internet Trade), the following tools are used:

– transformation language: ATL (Atlas Transformation Language);

– Execution Environment: ADT (Atlas Development Tool) with the Base Eclipse and the plug in for the various modeling languages.

The first task is to create the BPMN models of the cooperation between both sub-contractors: we call this model: TO BE top PIM (see Figure 7).

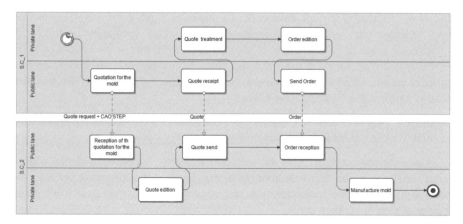

Figure 7. *TO BE top PIM*

The second task is to create the TO BE bottom PIM in order to introduce the mediation between the two sub-contractors. In the ISTA 3 the mediation is supported by the PETALS BUS (developed by the partner EBM WebSourcing) which controls all the exchanges, using the concepts of private and public processes.

5. Future works and conclusion

The development of the project has reached the following situation:

– the model of cooperation between sub-contractor 1 and sub-contractor 2 has been developed at the TO BE Bottom PIM level;

– the SEINE connectors are in development;

– the ontology for the I3rdG are in development and initial work has been developed for the Mediation.

In the next months the development of phase 3 will be terminated in order to produce the I3rdG solutions.

The implementation (phase 4) and the definition of performance indicators (phase 5) are planned for the first semester of 2011. An analysis of the impact in terms of organization and also on financial point of view will be performed to compare the I3rdG solutions and I2ndG solutions. The maintenance point of view will also be taken into consideration.

At the same time, change management will be considered and specific actions will be taken with the involved companies in order to help them transform their processes and their information system: training but also direct interactions in the day-to-day work are planned. This is a key issue for a successful integration of I3rdG and its dissemination through a network of companies. First, the involved companies may redefine part of their information system. This evolution is linked to adjustments made at business then process management, due to the impact of I3rdG on the way collaboration is achieved and partnerships defined. Second, when new partners are identified they also need to be involved in the same approach and also need to perform this Cultural Revolution.

ISTA 3 project is certainly one of the most advanced projects in the application of MDI/SOA in aeronautics industry.

Along the project by refining the search of solutions, we put in evidence a lot of hired problems as the transformation from one level to the following but also the need to define reverse transformation, the necessity to add information by going from one level to another, etc.

There is a strong interest from the SMEs which want to develop interoperability solutions on a flexible way at a low cost. One innovation, if we compare with other projects in the same domain, is to start at the Business level with a language understandable by the end users and to be able to assume the coherence along the various phases of development.

Members of the ISTA 3 project:

– Coordinator: GFI;

– Industrial case: MIPNET SAS (JTT, HACOMA), SYSMECA;

– IT supplier: EBM WebSourcing, GFI;

– Research Organizations: University Bordeaux 1, ESTIA (Bayonne), University of Nantes (LIANA), ENI Tarbes, EMAC (Albi), EC Lille;

– Vocational Education Organization: CNAM Pays de la Loire.

6. References

[Bourey et al., 2007] Bourey J.P., Grangel S.R, Doumeingts G., Berre A., "Report on Model Driven Interoperability", *INTEROP NoE Deliverable DTG2.3*, May 15th, 2007

[Chen, 2006] Chen D., "Enterprise Interoperability Framework", in *Proceedings of the EMOI'06 (3rd International Workshop on Enterprise Modelling and Ontologies for Interoperability)*, in connection with the 18th Conference on Advanced Information Systems Engineering, CAiSE'2006, Luxembourg, 2006.

[Chen et al., 2003] Chen D., Doumeingts G., "European initiatives to develop interoperability of enterprise applications–basic concepts, framework and roadmap", *Annual Reviews in Control 27*, 2003, p. 153–162

[Doumeingts et al., 2001] Doumeingts G., Ducq Y., Vallespir B., Kleinhans S., "Production Management and Enterprise Modelling", *Computer in Industry*, Vol. 42, N° 2, 2001, p. 245-263.

[Doumeingts *et al.*, 1993] Doumeingts G., Chen D., Vallespir B., Fénié P., Marcotte F., "GIM (GRAI Integrated Methodology) and its Evolutions - A Methodology to Design and Specify Advanced Manufacturing Systems", *DIISM 1993*, Tokyo, Japan, 1993, p. 101-120

[Doumeingts *et al.*, 1998] Doumeingts G., Vallespir B., Chen D., "GRAI Grid Decisional Modelling - In Handbook on Architecture of Information Systems", Edited by P. Bernus, K. Mertins, G. Schmith - *International Handbook on Information Systems*, Springer Verlag, 1998, p. 313-337.

[Grangel *et al.*, 2009] Grangel S.R., Bigand M., Bourey J.P., "UML Profiles for Transforming GRAI Decisional Models into UML Use Cases", *13th IFAC Symposium on Information Control Problems in Manufacturing*, (INCOM'09), Moscow, *Information Control Problems in Manufacturing*, Volume # 13, 2009.

[Lemrabet *et al.*, 2010] Lemrabet Y., Touzi J., Clin D., Bigand M., Bourey J.P., "Mapping of BPMN models into UML models using SoaML PROFILE", *8th InternationalConference of Modeling and Simulation - MOSIM'10* - May 10-12, 2010 - Hammamet – Tunisia.

Doctoral Symposium

Doctoral Symposium

Jenny A. Harding, Loughborough University, United Kingdom
J.A.Harding@lboro.ac.uk

Nicolas Boissel-Dallier, Frederik Bénaben, Hervé Pingaud, and Jean-Pierre Lorré: The Mediation Information System Engineering Project: Status and Perspectives
Ecole des Mines d'Albi-Carmaux, Petals Link

E.J.A. Folmer, P.H.W.M. Oude Luttighuis, and J. van Hillegersberg: Quality Measurement of Semantic Standards
TNO ICT, University of Twente, Novay

Brian Elvesæter and Arne-Jørgen Berre: Towards a Model-Driven and Role-Configurable Methodology Suite for Enterprise and Service-Oriented Interoperability
SINTEF ICT, University of Oslo

Wenxin Mu, Frederik Bénaben, and Hervé Pingaud: Mediation Information System Engineering: Business and Logic Characterization in Collaborative Situation
Ecole des Mines d'Albi-Carmaux

N. Khilwani, and Jenny A. Harding: Role of Semantic Web in the Changing Context of Enterprise Collaboration
Wolfson School of Mechanical and Manufacturing Engineering, Loughborough University

Barry A. Piorkowski, J. X. Gao: A Dynamic Knowledge Management Framework
Centre for Innovative Product Development, University of Greenwich

Doctoral Symposium Chair's Message

The I-ESA'10 Doctoral Symposium provided an excellent opportunity for research students working or training in any area of Interoperability for Enterprise Software and Applications to report on their research topics and work to date. It also provided a creative and constructive atmosphere for less experienced researchers to interact and discuss their research issues and ideas with both senior researchers and other Doctoral Symposium participants. The Doctoral Symposium was held during the I-ESA'10 pre-conference, on 12 April 2010.

PhD study is extremely interesting and rewarding, but it can also be stressful, challenging and at times lonely. Hence opportunities, such as the I-ESA Doctorial Symposium, which encourage young researchers to discuss their experiences and exchange ideas and views from different perspectives, are extremely valuable and should be encouraged. In particular, participants at this symposium commented that hearing about the experiences of a recently graduated researcher (Dr Alok Choudhary) was very useful. Participants also felt that learning about new ideas from new domains and consequently seeing different research methodologies were also useful experiences gained from the symposium.

The six papers presented show interoperability from a wide perspective. They also represent the work of researchers at very different stages of their PhD study, i.e. from the early stages of concept generation, to reports of completed implementations and experiments. Two papers introduce the concepts of Mediation Information System Engineering, as N. Boissel-Dallier considers the technical layer automation, from a platform independent model to a running mediator and W. Mu examines business and logic characterization in collaborative situations. The work of E.J.A. Folmer addresses quality measurement of semantic standards, aiming to provide a validated quality model for semantic standards and an operationalization of this model into measures which can be applied to the attributes of a semantic standard. B. Elvesaeter discusses his research towards a model-driven and role-configurable methodology suite for enterprise and service-oriented interoperability, and this research addresses various challenges, including how to map the flow of business logic and data to services providing the necessary functionality. The requirements of enterprise collaboration change at different stages of the life-cycle of a virtual collaboration and this topic has been addressed by N. Khilwani's paper which examines the role of the semantic web in the changing context of enterprise collaboration. The final paper, contributed by B.A. Piorkowski, considers a dynamic knowledge management framework, profiling people's capability and competency through face to face meeting content analysis. B.A. Piorkowski's paper was awarded the Best Paper Award.

Valuable contributions were also made to the symposium by posters presented by Zahid Usman, Najam Anjum, Mohammad Al-Awamieh, Shagloof Dahkil and Syed M Hasan. In closing, may I give my thanks to the symposium reviewers and to Sri Krishna Kumar for their help prior to and during the symposium. I also thank all contributors for letting me share in their interesting work and helping to make this a most interesting day for all.

Jenny A. Harding, *Loughborough University, United Kingdom*

The Mediation Information System Engineering Project: Status and Perspectives[1]

N. Boissel-Dallier*,** — **F. Bénaben*** — **H. Pingaud*** — **J.-P. Lorré****

* Ecole des Mines d'Albi-Carmaux
Route de Teillet
81000 Albi
France

** Petals Link
4 rue Amélie
31000 Toulouse
France

ABSTRACT. *The Mediation Information System Engineering (MISE) proposes a new model-driven approach to improve interoperability of enterprise information systems. This approach allows users to design a mediation information system to deal with exchanged data, services and collaborative processes. This article presents the MISE project and its assumptions in order to introduce a new PhD subject designed to improve agility of MIS technical layers. It proposes to use semantic matchmaking to make dynamic service orchestration and to automate message transformation.*

KEYWORDS: *interoperability, mediation, information system, MDA, semantic, ontology, SOA, assumptions, perspectives, PhD subject*

---

1 Publisher's note: sections of this paper are identical to the paper by Wenxin Mu *et al.* in this book. Both papers are included specifically by request of the editor.

1. Introduction

Enterprise Collaboration is a main stake of nowadays industrial ecosystem. The capacity of partners to collaborate easily is consequently a crucial requirement for enterprises. According to InterOp[2], interoperability is the *ability of a system or a product to work with other systems or products without special effort from the customer or user* [1].

According to Prof. Hervé Pingaud, Interoperability can be seen as the *ultimate collaborative maturity level* (of organization) adapted to integration, which can be seen as the *ultimate collaboration level* (of network).

1.1. *MISE project introduction*

In a collaborative context, the integration of industrial partners deeply depends on the ability of their Information Systems (IS) to interact efficiently. We consider that the IS contains the visible part of an enterprise. Our point is to study enterprise collaboration issues through ISs interoperability, while satisfying business requirements. Yet, one strong hypothesis we base our work on, is that partners' IS are supposed to follow the same conceptual logical architectural style: Service Oriented Architecture (SOA) [2].

This leads to a context where the each partner is able to contribute to the collaboration space through an interface that is a service whatever the level considered (computer independent or platform independent). Once this "philosophy" is defined, ISs interoperability may be supported through a mediation approach. According to [3], IS can be seen as a set of interacting data, services and processes, thus [4] and [5] propose the three following main interoperability functions: (i) conversion and delivery of data, (ii) management of applications (or services in a SOA context) and (iii) orchestration of collaborative processes.

Partners' ISs cannot natively assume those three functions (without a strong logic and technical standardization which seems to be too reducing). A Mediation Information System (MIS) seems to be a credible and pertinent way of supporting ISs interoperability [6].

Finally, the MIS should handle (i) knowledge about partners' data, (ii) a repository of partners' services and (iii) a collaborative process model that should be run and a workflow engine that enables to run it.

---

2 InterOp was a European Network of Excellence dedicated to Interoperability issues.

1.2. *General approach*

The global MIS design is based on model-driven concepts, i.e. a dive across abstraction levels (business, logic and technologic), using tools such as model transformation and ontology. Considering one particular collaborative situation, the proposed principle is to use the knowledge about collaboration (enterprises, roles, topology of the network, provided services, goals, etc.) to instantiate a network ontology. Deduction rules can be applied on this collaboration model to propose a model of Collaborative Process (CP) as Computer Independent Model (CIM) [7]. Collaborative process model is transferred into Platform Independent Model (PIM) by implementing transformation rules, defined in [8]. The PIM model has three views: service, information and process. Then, the Platform Specific Model (PSM) is built adding technical knowledge to PIM (e.g. Web Service descriptions). This logic model of MIS is specifically designed for an Enterprise Service Bus (ESB) technology. Finally, workflow and services are extracted from PSM model in order to configure and deploy MIS in an ESB.

2. MISE assumptions

2.1. *Assumptions and limits at business level*

First of all, the CIM collaborative process model covers mainly the operational level in enterprise business modeling. However, referring to ISO 9000:2000 recommendations, the decision level and support level should be considered. To complete the collaborative model, we should add some views (e.g. decision view, support view, risk management and information view).

Secondly, the MIT Process Handbook is used as a process knowledge repository to catch service definitions at different levels of granularity. After user has built a collaborative network model, business services are selected from an ontology, based on the MIT repository. However, this approach based on reusability leads to one problem: domain coverage of MIT Process Handbook knowledge limits MISE on process modeling capabilities as a single business service source.

2.2. *Assumptions and limits at the technical level*

During the CIM to PSM transformations, [8] makes the assumption that the link between BPMN business activities and available technical services is always possible and computerizable. Unfortunately, this assumption is correct only if each activity has one existing technical service linkable by name or other syntactic properties. Potential semantic problems are avoided. Information brought from PSM is supposed to be correct and clear enough to match web services.

Furthermore, [8] considers business activities and technical services as two resources with the same granularity. He only makes one to one connections. In concrete cases, these links are not enough to complete BPMN to SOA transformation and n to m relations should be inevitable.

In order to improve system agility and maturity, [9] adds a technical ontology containing functional (address, messages, etc.) and non-functional information (requirements, etc.) about existing services. Unfortunately, this service ontology is not based on a Semantic Web Services standard despite the fact that a lot of specifications are available and are close to our requirements. It does not promote interoperability, which is major goal in this project. Furthermore, the semantic matchmaking is manually performed and only existing technical services are usable.

In the technical level, [8] manages web services without taking heterogeneity of exchanged messages into account. For two consecutive services, he considers the output message of the first "sender" service to be similar to the input message expected by the second "receiver" service. When [9] improves the MIS design, he proposes to add interoperability service utilities called mediation services, which reduce message heterogeneity. For now, this feature is filled up interactively and rather manually with correspondences to point out all possible couples.

2.3. *Assumptions and limits on the general approach*

As in most classical model-driven architecture studies, the system is put into practice using a series of top-down transformations from the Collaborative Process Model to the ESB configuration. Each transformation brings additional information to the system in order to reach the final targeted implementation.

[8] makes a first MIS design for which the top-down assumption is straightforward. No feedback has been introduced, however information coming from low level could enhance higher levels and bottom-up transformations have to be investigated. It leads to the conclusion that partners have to restart the whole conception design phase in case of process changes, of execution problems (e.g. missing service) or if the final system does not meet all their initial requirements.

[9] tries to improve MIS reengineering capabilities. In one hand, he screens possible problems in order to determine where design could be restarted. For example, it avoids restarting the whole process in case of small technical problem. In the other hand, he adds flexibility features: (i) it allows users to select lately some services chosen during the design phase. Then, the final decision is done during the execution. That is called *delayed choice*. (ii) It enables users to leave some activity

undefined during the design time and then build the process on the fly. This is *delayed process design*.

3. Positioning and expected contribution

Until now, semantic information has mainly been limited to high level (from CP to CIM) and business syntactic description frequently appears as semantically meaningful for subsequent levels. But only syntactic data are passed on the CIM to PIM transformation. That brings the technical problems we cited above. In order to resolve the automation of message adaptation and improve matching between business activities and technical services (from manually one to one to automatic n to m matching), the contribution of semantics in lower level models is under study and becomes a focus of our research.

Most of the research about the dynamic orchestration of services turns toward the use of semantics [11]. Three phases are generally performed: (i) knowledge modeling. This generally involves the creation of knowledge bases (called ontologies) which represent all concepts within a domain and the relationships between those concepts [12]. (ii) Incorporating semantics into models involved in transformation processes. Here, we have to add knowledge to technical services and to a higher level (to determine). To bring semantics on web services, one standard among many such as SAWSDL, OWL-S, WSMO or WSMO-Lite seems to support efficiently development of Semantic Web Services [13]. (iii) Using semantic information to match services and messages. It is a major challenge in MIS design to find correspondences between business activities and real web services as well as to configure messages transformations on the fly using semantic matchmakers.

This new PhD subject proposes to improve the technical level of MIS with semantic use. This study aims to automate, maybe partially, both PIM to PSM transformation and message transformation thanks to existing standards. This new evolution of MIS aims to improve mediator agility adding dynamic orchestration.

On the one hand, semantics brings knowledge to syntactic service definition and allows reasoning on it. Considering possible semantic annotations from higher levels, it becomes possible to link business activities to existing services thanks to semantic similarity measures. Some existing service ontologies enable us to semantically describe the internal process of web services which allows us to make n to m matchmaking.

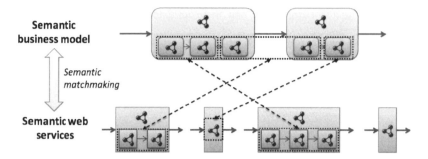

Figure 1. *Semantic matchmaking using internal semantic descriptions*

On the other hand, all service ontology frameworks cited below enable the semantic description of messages. It allows message semantic matchmaking and can be used to compare service input and output in order to make dynamic transformation possible. This automated transformation will eventually be included in the mediator and replace manual transformation.

Figure 2. *Dynamic message transformation using semantic annotations*

Both evolutions must be designed to improve mediator agility, completing *delayed choice* and *process design* mechanisms.

4. Conclusion

MISE promotes an interoperability design tool to manage data exchange, services sharing and dynamic process orchestrations. The engineering is based on a four-step process: (i) build collaborative network and processes, (ii) transfer collaborative process model into PIM, (iii) gather technical information and transfer PIM to PSM and (iv) transfer PSM to a target software system.

However, assumptions made at the business level, technical level and general approach were studied and discussed during a first experiment. The objective of this PhD subject is to improve the technical layer automation, from PIM model to running mediator.

5. References

[1] Konstantas D, Bourrières JP, Léonard M, Boudjlida N, *Interoperability of Enterprise Software and Applications. I-ESA'05* pp. v-vi. Springer, Geneva, Switzerland (2005)

[2] Vernadat F, "Interoperable enterprise systems: architecture and methods", Plenary lecture, *IFAC/INCOM Conference*, Saint-Etienne (2006)

[3] Morley C, Hugues J, Leblanc B, *UML pour l'analyse d'un système d'information*, 2nd edition, Dunod, France (2002)

[4] Bénaben F, Touzi J, Rajsiri V, Pingaud H, *Collaborative Information System Design. AIM 2006 Information Systems and Collaboration: State of the Art and Perspectives*, pp 281-296. GI-Edition, Lecture Notes in Informatics (2006)

[5] Aubert B, Dussart A, SI Inter-Organisationnels. CIRANO Bourgogne report (2002)

[6] Bénaben F, Pingaud H, "The MISE Project: A First Experience in Mediation Information System Engineering", *Information Systems: People, Organizations, Institutions, and Technologies*, 2010. p. 399-406

[7] Rajsiri V, Lorré JP, Bénaben F, Pingaud H, "Knowledge-based system for collaborative process specification", Special issue of *CII (Computers in Industry)*, Elsevier (2009)

[8] Touzi J, Bénaben F, Pingaud H, Lorré JP, "A Model-Driven approach for Collaborative Service-Oriented Architecture design", Special issue of *IJPE (International Journal of Production Economics)*, Elsevier (2008)

[9] Truptil S, Bénaben F, Couget P, Lauras M, Chapurlat V, Pingaud H, "Interoperability of information systems in crisis management: Crisis modeling and metamodeling", *Proceeding of I-ESA 2008: Enterprise Interoperability III*, Berlin, Germany (2008)

[11] Preist C, "Goal and Vision: Combining Web Services with Semantic Web Technology", *Semantic Web Services: Concepts, Technologies and Applications*, Springer-Verlag, pp. 159-178 (2008)

[12] Milton N, "Knowledge Technologies", *Polimetrica*, Publishing Studies series, Vol. 3 (2008)

[13] Lausen L, Lara R, Polleres A, de Bruijn J, Roman D, "Description: Semantic Annotation for Web Services", *Semantic Web Services: Concepts, Technologies and Applications*, Springer-Verlag, pp. 179-209 (2008)

Quality Measurement of Semantic Standards

E.J.A. Folmer*'** — P.H.W.M. Oude Luttighuis*** — J. van Hillegersberg**

* TNO ICT
Colosseum 27, 7521 PV, Enschede
The Netherlands

** University of Twente
PO Box 217, 7500 AE, Enschede
The Netherlands

*** Novay
PO Box 589, 7500 AN, Enschede
The Netherlands

ABSTRACT. *Quality of semantic standards is not adressed in current research while there is an explicit need from standard developers. The business importance is evident since quality of standards will have an impact on its diffusion and achieved interoperability in practice. An instrument to measure the quality of semantic standards is designed to contribute to the knowledge domain, standards developers and might ultimately lead to improved interoperability. This instrument is iteratively designed with multiple case studies. This paper describes the rationale and research design, as well as current status and future plans.*

KEYWORDS: *quality, semantic, standards, interoperability*

1. Problem description

Little scientific literature addresses the issue of the quality of semantic standards (Folmer, Berends, Oude Luttighuis, & Van Hillegersberg, 2009). Sherif and Egyedi state that their paper (Sherif, Egyedi, & Jakobs, 2005) is the first to address standards quality, albeit for technical standards. Regarding semantic standards, Markus asserts that the quality of a standard correlates with the adoption of that standard: "The success of Vertical Information Systems standards diffusion is affected by the technical content of the developed standard, ..." (Markus, Steinfield, Wigand, & Minton, 2006). To our knowledge, in public policy circles, the quality of standards is mentioned for the first time in a whitepaper of the European Commission in 2009, where it is stated as a policy goal to "increase the quality, coherence and consistency of ICT standards" (Modernising ICT Standardisation in the EU - The Way Forward, 2009). In the meantime within the EU standardization has become top priority in order to support the stabilization of a common market and the unification of Europe (Hommels, Schueler, & Fickers, 2008). Standards are often seen as a means to achieve the interoperability needed for social and economic goals, for example by the Dutch government (The Netherlands Open in Connection - An action plan for the use of Open Standards and Open Source Software in the public and semi-public sector, 2007). An example of economic relevance is the well documented study of the costs of imperfect interoperability estimated at $1 billion in the US automobile sector (Brunnermeier & Martin, 2002).

2. Goal and research questions

The main goal of this study is to build an instrument to measure the quality of semantic standards in order to make the quality of standards transparent. To be able to fulfil this goal, research questions will be answered, amongst others:
 – What is the state of the art on quality measurement of semantic standards?
 – What are the requirements for the instrument?
 – What constitutes a semantic standard?
 – What characteristics determine the quality of the standard?
 – How can the quality characteristics be instrumentalized?

3. Research method

To be able to answer the research questions we categorized our research in order to be able to design our research. The summary of the characteristics is as follows:
 – research type: design science in IS research;

– research epistemology: interpretive;

– research design: mixed methods;

– research methods/approaches: several, including focus groups, workshops, surveys and case studies.

The new and innovative design of an artefact which solves a wicked problem is typically design science research (Hevner, March, Park, & Ram, 2004). A structured literature review has been used to prove the innovative character, while a survey was used for identification of the wicked problem. This is the first phase of the study which shows the applicability of design science research.

The second phase is the actual design and evaluation according in line with design science, and is graphically depicted in Figure 1.

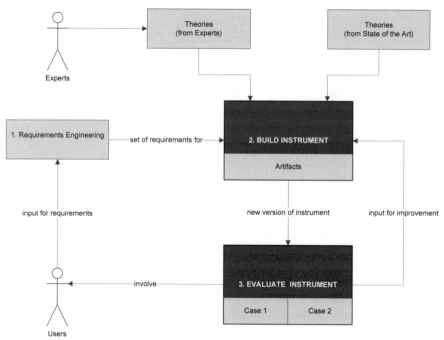

Figure 1. *Overall research design*

A state-of-the-art analysis was performed on the current status of the knowledge base to identify constructs to build on. Workshops and expert sessions were used for gathering requirements for the desired solution. The iterative design will consist of minimal two design cycles, consisting of one case study for evaluation purposes within each design cycle.

4. Problem validation

The results of the structured literature review show that semantic standards are poorly addressed in the top 25 information system and management journals (Folmer *et al.*, 2009). The research labels the quality of semantic standards topic as a research gap in the current knowledge base.

Representatives from semantic Standard Development Organizations (SDOs) largely support the hypothesis that the quality of their standards can be improved, just as they support the hypothesis that quality improvement of their standard might lead to improved interoperability in practice. These hypotheses were tested in a survey among 34 international semantic SDOs, including GS1, HL7, hr-XML, Papinet, amongst others (Folmer, Oude Luttighuis, & Van Hillegersberg, 2010).

In order to improve the quality of their standards, semantic SDOs might use an instrument to measure the quality and create transparency about the quality. If developed 81% of the respondents are interested in using the instrument (Folmer, Oude Luttighuis *et al.*, 2010).

By performing this structured literature review and survey, we proved our research to address both research and a business gap.

5. State of the art

Although quality of semantic standards defines a research gap, both standardization and quality are two well developed knowledge areas. The state-of the art analysis helps us to define our concepts, first of all the notion of semantic standards, which includes business transaction standards, ontologies, vocabularies, messaging standards, vertical industry standards, and many more terms. Often, semantic standards include XML-based syntax, but the value of the standard is its description of the meaning of data and process information to achieve semantic interoperability. Semantic standards can focus on a single industry sector or purport to be applicable across sectors (Steinfield, Wigand, Markus, & Minton, 2007).

Quality is defined as fitness for use (Juran & Gryna, 1988), which in our context defines quality of the standard as its ability to achieve the intended purpose of the standard. For semantic standards this means the quality is the fitness for achieving semantic interoperability. This implies that quality deals with both intrinsic aspects (the specification) and situational aspects (external environment) of the standard.

Measurement is defined by ISO (ISO/IEC, 1984) as a set of operations with the object of determining a value of a quantity. Our measurement instrument is a tool that supports the determination of values of quality aspects of the semantic standard at hand.

In the design phase, the state of the art analysis is used for identification of quality aspects, which were found, but only in a scattered and probably partial sense, and focusing on particular popular subtopics in literature, like the standardization process. Interesting is the literature about quality from the software engineering domain. We also found a meta language for quality of software (Garcia *et al.*, 2009) to be useful in the semantic standards domain as well.

6. The design process

Our design starting point has been a requirements engineering study among potential users, performed in two workshops. The intended user is described as the expert from an SDO who wants to improve the standard. The identified requirements are leading in the design process. The top goal "To support semantic SDO's in developing high quality standards" has been decomposed into three level-two goals, which have been further decomposed:

– useful for different SDOs: the instrument should be sufficiently generic to be used by many semantic SDOs;

– able to efficiently determine the quality and give improvement suggestions: it should be efficient to use, but also give improvement suggestions to the user;

– have useable results for SDOs: the outcome should be useful and valuable for SDO's.

Based on the full set of requirements, structured in a goal-tree, our design started by identifying the main construction of the instrument. This has led to the following structure and representation of the instrument Quality Measurement of Semantic Standard (iQMSS):

instrument Quality Measurement of Semantic Standards (iQMSS)

		Specification Quality Model Semantic Standard (QM SS)	Specification Semantic Standard Model (SSM)	Implementation
Model of	M2	1. Quality Language (QL)	I. SS Language (SSL)	A. Development Environment
	M1	2. Generic QMSS	II. Generic SSM	B. GMI Generic Model Implementation
Customization of	M1	3. Customized QMSS	III. Customized SSM	C. SMI Customized Model Implementation
Model of	M0	4. Measurement Result	IV. Semantic Standard	D. Measurement Result Report

Table 1. *Constructs of instrument*

We distinguished three different subdomains in the design of iQMSS: the quality model and the semantic standard model, which both need implementation to be instrumentalized. Each of these span different levels, based on "model of" relation or generalization specilization relation. The type of relation and M-levels according to the Model Driven Architecture (Kleppe, Warmer, & Bast, 2003) are presented in the table.

Based on the requirements, it was determined that there is a need for a general version of the instrument, but to be valuable it needs to be specialized for each standard as subject for the measurement.

Based on the state-of-the-art analysis, it was decided to use the work of SMM (Software Measurement Metamodel) and SMML (Software Measurement Modelling Language) (García et al., 2006; Garcia et al., 2009) as Quality Language (QL) and Semantic Standard Language (SSL) on the M2 level. The SMM language is based on a set of existing ISO definitions for many concepts relevant in a quality model, and although designed for software it fits the domain of semantic standards as well.

First, the Semantic Standard Model (SSM) is addressed before the actual quality model (QMSS) is developed. The SSM should indicate what the domain of the standard is, it identifies the attributes of the standard that form the point of action for the quality instrument. Every measurable quality aspect of the standard should be targeted at some attribute in SSM. In fact, the SSM defines a semantic standard in detailed.

7. Iterative design cycles

The iterative nature of our design resulted in an early first version of the the the Quality Model for Semantic Standard (QMSS), and a first explorative case study (Folmer, Van Bekkum, Oude Luttighuis, & Van Hillegersberg, 2010).

The first design uses several sources, particularly from ISO 9126 (ISO/IEC, 2001), which proved to be a valuable fundament for QMSS. At the highest level, the QMSS structures the quality aspects in the categories: Functionality, Reliability, Usability, Portability, Maintainability, Adoptability and Openness. A first explorative case study was performed for the SETU standard, a semantic standard for the temporary staffing industry, and has led to an extensive list of improvement suggestions for the next design cycle of the instrument. In the next design cycles, the QMSS will be improved and evaluated, but also the emphasis will shift to building and evaluating the implementation of the models (iQMSS).

8. Conclusion and further research

Currently, the first design cycle has been completed, but several more are needed. Further work needs to be done on the state-of-the-art analysis, including reflection on the original problem statement and project plan for possible alterations based on the new knowledge. The current version of the SSM requires validation, which will be done using the literature found in the state-of-the-art analysis. In the next design cycles, experts will be consulted for identifying more quality aspects and determining how to measure them. The implementation of the models in tooling is also a next step. The evaluation of the final design cycle, as part of this study, will include a survey among the same participants from the problem statement survey. Thus, we return to our original proposition and fundament of design science research: solving real-life problems.

The main research contribution of this study will be:

– the validated quality model for semantic standards;

– an operationalization of this model into measures, performed on the attributes of a semantic standard.

Insight into their quality may help improve semantic standards. Ultimately, this may lead to improved interoperability and, from that, the achievement of economic and societal goals.

9. References

Brunnermeier, S. B., & Martin, S. A. (2002). "Interoperability costs in the US automotive supply chain". *Supply Chain Management, 7*(2), 71-82.

Folmer, E., Berends, W., Oude Luttighuis, P., & Van Hillegersberg, J. (2009). "Top IS research on quality of transaction standards, a structured literature review to identify a research gap". Paper presented at the *6th International Conference on Standardization and Innovation in Information Technology*, Tokyo, Japan.

Folmer, E., Oude Luttighuis, P., & Van Hillegersberg, J. (2010). *Quality of Semantic Standards Needs Improvement; A Survey Among 34 Semantic Standards.* forthcoming

Folmer, E., Van Bekkum, M., Oude Luttighuis, P., & Van Hillegersberg, J. (2010). *The Quality Measurement of Semantic Standards; The Case of the SETU Standard for the Dutch Government.* forthcoming.

García, F., Bertoa, M. F., Calero, C., Vallecillo, A., Ruíz, F., Piattini, M., *et al.* (2006). "Towards a consistent terminology for software measurement". *Information and Software Technology, 48*(8), 631-644.

Garcia, F., Ruiz, F., Calero, C., Bertoa, M. F., Vallecillo, A., Mora, B., *et al.* (2009). "Effective use of ontologies in software measurement". *The Knowledge Engineering Review, 24*(Special Issue 01), 23-40.

Hevner, A. R., March, S. T., Park, J., & Ram, S. (2004). "Design science in information systems research". *MIS Quarterly: Management Information Systems, 28*(1), 75-105.

Hommels, A., Schueler, J., & Fickers, A. (2008). "The Complexity of Negotiating Technical Standards". In A. Hommels, J. Schueler & A. Fickers (Eds.), *Bargaining Norms Arguing Standards* (pp. 12-16). The Hague: STT.

ISO/IEC. (1984). *International vocabulary of basic and general terms in metrology.*

ISO/IEC. (2001). *ISO/IEC 9126-1 Software engineering - Product quality - Part 1: Quality model.*

Juran, J. M., & Gryna, F. M. (Eds.). (1988). *Juran's Quality Control Handbook* (4th edition ed.): McGraw-Hill.

Kleppe, A., G. , Warmer, J., & Bast, W. (2003). *MDA Explained: The Model Driven Architecture: Practice and Promise*: Addison-Wesley Longman Publishing Co., Inc.

Markus, M. L., Steinfield, C. W., Wigand, R. T., & Minton, G. (2006). "Industry-wide Information Systems standardization as collective action: The case of U.S. residential mortgage industry". *MIS Quarterly, 30*, 439-465.

Modernising ICT Standardisation in the EU - The Way Forward. (2009). Retrieved 2010-01-20. from http://ec.europa.eu/enterprise/newsroom/cf/document.cfm?action=display&doc_id=3152&userservice_id=1&request.id=0.

The Netherlands Open in Connection - An Action Plan for the Use of Open Standards and Open Source Software in the Public and Semi-public Sector. (2007). Retrieved 2010-01-20. from http://appz.ez.nl/publicaties/pdfs/07ET15.pdf.

Sherif, M. H., Egyedi, T. M., & Jakobs, K. (2005). "Standards of quality and quality of standards for telecommunications and information technologies". Paper presented at the *Proceedings of the 4th International Conference on Standardization and Innovation in Information Technology*, 2005, Geneva.

Steinfield, C. W., Wigand, R. T., Markus, M. L., & Minton, G. (2007). "Promoting e-business through vertical IS standards: lessons from the US home mortgage industry". In S. Greenstein & V. Stango (Eds.), *Standards and Public Policy* (pp. 160-207). Cambridge: Cambridge University Press.

Towards a Model-Driven and Role-Configurable Methodology Suite for Enterprise and Service-Oriented Interoperability

Brian Elvesæter*,** — **Arne-Jørgen Berre*,****

* SINTEF ICT
P. O. Box 124 Blindern
N-0314 Oslo
Norway

** University of Oslo
Department of Informatics
P. O. Box 1080 Blindern
N-0316 Oslo
Norway

ABSTRACT. *Service-orientation has been established as the dominating design principle of modern IT systems. Designing service-oriented systems involves different stakeholders who collaborate within the enterprise and requires a methodology suite that supports team-based development. This paper presents a PhD topic that aims to define the architecture and implement a tool-supported methodology suite that will support collaboration between the central roles and stakeholders involved in designing interoperable enterprise systems. The work will be based on a model-driven and service-oriented approach. The methodology suite will implement a knowledge base of reusable method components that can be configured to support the different roles and stakeholders. The work will in particular focus on the alignment between business models and IT architectures.*

KEYWORDS: *model-driven, methodology, service-oriented, interoperability*

1. Problem description

System interoperability is a growing interest area, because of the continuously growing need of integration of new, legacy and evolving systems. Enterprises today face many challenges related to lack of interoperability. Enterprises need to adapt more quickly to changes in the business and economic market and are required to become more responsive to customer needs. Although enterprises are heavily dependent on information technology (IT) solutions in their day-to-day business operations, the solutions are often inflexible and difficult to adapt to meet the requirements of those changing enterprises [1].

Service-orientation has been established as the dominating design principle of modern IT systems. The increasing popularity of service-oriented architecture (SOA) technologies relies on its ability to solving interoperability problems in multiple domains. SOA does not change the functionality of a product, but offers a new point of view that allows more reuse and flexible composition. SOA models are closer to business models and thus reflect business goals in a way that allows easier composition and enactment. However, there are several SOA implementations tied to different technologies. These implementations are typically specified at a low level of abstraction containing many technical details. The implication of this is that business requirements are often intertwined with the final specification, constraining the evolution of business requirements and SOA implementations. Furthermore, each technology platform implies the use of different approaches to solve the same problem.

Modeling is now an integrated part of software engineering approaches. Business process models are widely used to describe how work is done within an organization, while various product models describe what is done. Various approaches based on model-driven engineering (MDE) concepts, such as the OMG Model Driven Architecture (MDA) [2] and related efforts on domain-specific languages have gained much popularity. The design and implementation of SOA should benefit from the advances in the model-driven engineering approach, e.g. allowing the specification of both a business and technical view of SOA, supporting business to IT model refinement, and mapping to different technology platforms. In this context, some main challenges are:

– How to map the flow of business logic and data to services providing the needed functionality in a platform-independent way?

– How to integrate the various models describing goals, processes, requirements, data and services in a common model architecture that can also be adapted to individual projects and their implementation environment?

– How to manage such models and provide links between them that can be used for service composition or managing changes?

2. Research proposal

Designing SOAs at the enterprise level involves several different stakeholders within the enterprise. Model-driven engineering (MDE) frameworks can be used to partition the architecture of a system into several visual models at different abstraction levels subject to the concerns of the stakeholders. This allows important decisions regarding integration and interoperability to be made at the most appropriate level and by the best suited and knowledgeable people. The models can be formalized and expressed in visual modeling languages. A methodology suite aims to provide guidelines for how to develop the different kinds of models recommended for SOA. The models contribute to the understanding and specification of the system or services to be integrated or developed. Some models provide the basis for automated code generation.

The PhD research will further study the alignment between enterprise models and IT models and architect a tool-supported methodology suite to support the design of interoperable enterprise services. The PhD topic continues the methodology research from the ATHENA Interoperability Framework [3]. The methodology suite will be developed as an interactive and Web-based knowledge portal. Such a portal will provide a collaboration space where relevant tools and services can be offered to the users. Methodology guidelines will be made available as configurable services on a method engineering platform. The Web-based portal will adopt a service-oriented architecture which defines a collaboration infrastructure supporting the lifecycle of interoperability projects.

The problem of enterprise interoperability is complex and requires support from many methods to be resolved. Which methods are needed depends on the type of system. The future of systems engineering will not see just one approach but a multitude of approaches depending on the type of system and the degree of reuse of solutions. Future systems will range from global data collection, analysis and presentation to dynamic systems for mass-customized product design. We postulate that it is impossible to provide one universal approach and methodology for interoperability problem solving. We therefore propose to define a knowledge base of reusable method components each of them addressing one or more specific interoperability problems that can be configured into a full methodology supporting the multiple roles and stakeholders involved in designing enterprise systems.

3. Research method

State-of-the-art studies will be carried out in national and European research projects that will identify and describe relevant technologies, techniques and mechanisms. The main PhD work will follow an iterative research cycle applied to a real-life case study. One or more industry use case scenarios focusing on tool-supported methodology for IT architectures and enterprise interoperability will be established related to Integration Operations (IO) in the Oil & Gas industry sector.

The Norwegian Oil Industry Association (OLF) has defined the term Integrated Operations (IO) as "real time data onshore from offshore fields and new integrated work processes" [4]. The technical implication from IO is an increased exchange of information across geographical and organizational boundaries, internally and externally. New, interoperable IT solutions and standards are needed for this information exchange to be successful.

The results of the state-of-the-art analysis together with an analysis of the industry requirements will provide the basis for further work. This work will define the architecture of the methodology suite. The methodology suite will be incrementally developed following the iterative research cycle. In order to be successfully adopted, the methodology should guide companies in selecting the best approaches for their interoperability needs. For each approach, a methodology should describe:

– which roles are involved in the project (organization perspective);

– which tasks they perform in which order (process perspective);

– which tools they use for each task (infrastructure perspective);

– what the resulting artefacts and solutions are (product perspective).

The work will define and develop concepts and languages to describe the composition (assembly) and role-configuration of methodologies. We will define and develop method components for supporting various roles involved in enterprise SOA interoperability that will be described according to the concepts and languages defined. Finally, we will develop prototype tools to validate, illustrate and test the concepts, languages, methods and services. The prototype will make use of and propose and implement extensions to the Eclipse Process Framework (EPF) [5]. EPF is an open-source Eclipse project that provides an extensible framework and exemplary tools for software process engineering. EPF implements the Software Process Engineering Metamodel (SPEM), which defines typical concepts of a process (process, phase, role, model, etc.) that can be used to construct models that describe software engineering process.

4. Expected contributions

The PhD ideas presented in this paper have been partially researched in the European research project SHAPE (ICT-2007-216408) [6] with the development of a tool-supported methodology framework for SOA in the Eclipse Process Framework (EPF). The overall aim of the project is to develop the foundations for the model-driven development of service-oriented system landscapes. The methodology framework is centred around the OMG MDA specifications Business Process Modeling Notation (BPMN) version 2.0 [7] and Service oriented architecture Modeling Language (SoaML) [8]. Both of these standards are currently in their finalization phase and there is ongoing harmonization of the service-oriented concepts defined in the specifications.

The PhD work will continue to build on the research results from the ATHENA Interoperability Framework and the SHAPE Methodology for SOA. The expected contributions of the PhD research are:

– to provide guidelines and method components for how MDE principles and MDA technologies should be applied to develop interoperable service-oriented systems;

– to provide a set of method components covering the SOA development lifecycle that lets you assemble and configure situational methodologies, with special focus on integration and interoperability issues, and alignment of business models and IT models; and

– to provide an open-source prototype implementation of a customizable and role-configurable method engineering platform.

5. References

[1] D. P. Truex, R. Baskerville, and H. Klein, "Growing Systems in Emergent Organizations", *Communications of the ACM*, vol. 42, no. 8, pp. 117-123, 1999.

[2] OMG, "OMG Model Driven Architecture", *Object Management Group* (OMG). http://www.omg.org/mda (last visited 2010).

[3] A.-J. Berre, B. Elvesæter, N. Figay, C. Guglielmina, S. G. Johnsen, D. Karlsen, and S. Lippe, "The ATHENA Interoperability Framework", in *Proc. of the 3rd International Conference on Interoperability for Enterprise Software and Applications (I-ESA'07)*, Madeira, Portugal, 2007, Enterprise Interoperability II, Springer, pp. 569-580.

[4] OLF, "Integrated Operations and the Oil & Gas Ontology", *OLF*, 2007. http://www.olf.no/getfile.php/zKonvertert/www.olf.no/Rapporter/Dokumenter/070919%20IO%20and%20Ontology%20-%20Brosjyre.pdf

[5] Eclipse.org, "Eclipse Process Framework Project (EPF)". http://www.eclipse.org/epf/ (last visited 2010).

[6] SHAPE, "SHAPE Home Page", SHAPE STREP. http://www.shape-project.eu

[7] OMG, "Business Process Model and Notation (BPMN), FTF Beta 1 for Version 2.0", Object Management Group, OMG Document dtc/2009-08-14, August 2009. http://www.omg.org/spec/BPMN/2.0/Beta1/PDF/

[8] OMG, "Service oriented architecture Modeling Language (SoaML), FTF Beta 1", Object Management Group, OMG Document ptc/2009-04-01, April 2009. http://www.omg.org/spec/SoaML/1.0/Beta1/PDF/

Mediation Information System Engineering: Business and Logic Characterization in a Collaborative Situation[1]

W. Mu* — F. Bénaben* — H. Pingaud*

* Ecole des Mines d'Albi-Carmaux
Route de Teillet
81000 Albi
France

ABSTRACT. *The Mediation Information System Engineering (MISE) proposes a new model-driven approach to improve interoperability of enterprises information systems. This approach allows users to design a mediation information system to deal with data exchange, services and collaborative processes. However, there are three assumptions in business level in the MISE project. These assumptions are mainly about collaboration knowledge limitation and the linear engineering process. In order to solve these assumptions, a PhD subject has been proposed to improve characterization in a collaborative situation by adding different views.*

KEYWORDS: *interoperability, mediation, MDA, ontology, collaborative process, SOA, limits, assumptions*

1 Publisher's note: sections of this paper are identical to the paper by Nicolas Boissel-Dallier *et al.* in this book. Both papers are included specifically by request of the editor.

1. Introduction

Enterprises operate in an environment where markets are more open, globalized and competitive. Changes in market conditions oblige enterprises to become involved in various kinds of industrial networks in order to maintain their business efficiency. The efficiency of networked enterprises is determined by the speed and accuracy with which information can be managed and exchanged among the business partners. Enterprise Collaboration is a main stake of the industrial ecosystem nowadays. The capacity of partners to collaborate easily is consequently a crucial requirement for enterprises.

According to InterOp (InterOp was a European Network of Excellence dedicated to Interoperability issues), interoperability is the ability of a system or a product to work with other systems or products without special effort from the customer or user [1]. Interoperability can also be seen as the ultimate collaborative maturity level (of organization) adapted to integration, which can be seen as the ultimate collaboration level (of network).

1.1. *MISE project introduction*

Considering the fact that Information System (IS) is the visible part of an enterprise, our point is to tackle enterprises collaboration issue through ISs interoperability satisfying the business requirements. Yet, one strong hypothesis we base our work on is that partners' IS are supposed to follow the same conceptual logical architectural style: Service Oriented Architecture (SOA) [2]. This leads to a context where each partner is able to contribute to the collaboration space through interfaces that are its services whatever the level considered (computer-independent or platform-independent). Once this "philosophy" is defined, ISs interoperability may be supported through a mediation approach. According to [3], IS can be seen as a set of interacting data, services and processes, thus [4] and [5] propose the three following main interoperability functions:

- conversion and delivery of data;
- management of applications (or services in a SOA context);
- orchestration of collaborative process.

Partners' ISs cannot natively assume these three functions (without a strong logic and technical standardization which seems to be too reducing). A Mediation Information System (MIS) seems to be a credible and pertinent way of supporting ISs interoperability [6].

Finally, the MIS should be able to deal with the three functions identified below among a set of SOA partners' ISs. It should handle (i) knowledge about partners' data, (ii) a repository of partners' services and (iii) a collaborative process model that should be run and a workflow engine that enables us to run it.

1.2. *General approach*

The global MIS design is based on model-driven concepts, i.e. a dive across abstraction levels (business, logic and technologic), using tools such as model transformation and ontology. Considering one particular collaborative situation, the proposed principle is to use the knowledge about collaboration (enterprises involved, roles, topology of the network, services provided, goals, etc.) to instantiate a network ontology. Deduction rules can be applied on this collaboration model to propose a collaborative process (CP) model such as Computer Independent Model (CIM). This part of work has been achieved by Rajsiri in [7]. Extracting the knowledge embedded into this CP model, model morphism mechanisms can be applied (based on CP and MIS metamodels) in order to propose a model of the logic architecture of the adequate MIS as Platform-Independent Model (PIM). This part of the work is implemented by Jihed in [8] and [9]. Finally, using this logic model of MIS, a final step of transformation mechanism can be executed in order to obtain a technological configuration of the dedicated MIS as Platform Specific Model (PSM) specifically for an Enterprise Service Bus (ESB) technology. This part of work is presented in Wenxin's mister report and [10].

2. MISE assumptions at business level

In this section, assumptions concerning business level (CIM) are presented. The assumptions are separated into three parts.

First of all, the limits about collaborative knowledge are discussed. The CIM collaborative process model is an operational process model. Collaborative process model covers mainly the operational level in enterprise business modeling. However, referring to the ISO 9000:2000 recommendations, the decision level and support level should be considered. In order to make sure the collaborative model contains all the collaborative information, more information should be added as different views (for example, decision view, support view and information view).

Furthermore, the MISE model-driven approach is a linear engineering process. As such, there are two problems. On the one hand, if one part of one model in the model transformation chain is changed, the whole remaining part of the chain must be driven again. On the other hand, if one modeling tool does not work, the whole chain does not work. To solve the problem, we decided to overcome the limitations induced by the CIM and PIM segregations. A concept of model container (collaborative model) is under study. The container collects CIM and PIM definitions together with all the expected complementary collaborative knowledge. A set of extractive rules could be defined to get CIM and PIM from the container.

Last but not least, the MIT Process Handbook is used as a process knowledge repository to catch definitions of services at different levels of granularity. Once the user has built a collaborative network model, business services are selected from a special version of the MIT repositories available as an ontology.

The CIM process could choose useful services to build its collaborative process model. This approach, based on reusability, leads to two problems. Firstly, the collaborative process model is generally not focused on specific enterprises or organizations. Secondly, limits of MIT Process Handbook knowledge became limits of MISE on process modeling capabilities.

3. PhD subject: business and logic characterization in a collaborative situation

To deal with the assumptions introduced in section 2.1, a PhD subject has been proposed. In this subject, three tasks have been defined:

– define a collaboration situation (CS) framework with three dimensions;

– define meta-models covering all the cubes in the collaboration situation framework and define transformation rules between meta-models;

– develop a software tool to implement models' development and transformation.

In the first task, a collaborative framework should contain and classify all the information needed in collaborative situation and the knowledge extracted from other sources needed in collaborative situation, and will give the opportunity to manage this knowledge in a more integrated manner. The framework has been designed at the beginning of this PhD subject with CS management, CS lifecycle and CS element (as shown in Figure 1 collaboration situation framework).

Secondly, several modeling languages will be chosen to build meta-models. These meta-models cover all the framework. Each meta-model could cover one or more cubes. In order to implement transformation rules between these meta-models, a large meta-model container (one covering meta-model or one ontology) needs to be designed (as shown in Figure 1 meta-models and meta-model container design).

Thirdly, if modeling capabilities evolve, by consequence transformation rules between different models will also need to evolve. Evolution of the MISE prototype platform has to be performed. Three steps have been shown in Figure 1.

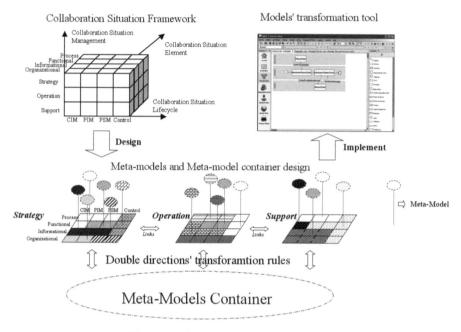

Figure 1. *PhD subject solution global map*

The Olina-Computer store example has been used to illustrate two steps of the proposition (focus on collaboration situation element dimension in collaboration situation framework, furthermore this example is only an intermediate illustration of collaboration model, it is not the final result): build collaborative model into the unified framework and extract the collaborative process. The example is based on a simple collaborative goal: a trade transaction between a seller and a buyer. Olina is the buyer. She would like to buy a new notebook from the computer store (seller actor).

Step1: emancipation of the collaborative model. The collaborative model may be conceived as shown in Figure 2. The collaborative model not only covers operational process in the functional view, but also decision, resource, organization and information in other viewpoints. The collaborative model is the whole container (section 2.1 assumption No. 2). CIM and PIM representations could be extracted from this collaborative model inside the unified framework. Linking this container with external knowledge sources (like process repositories) will be a determining quality.

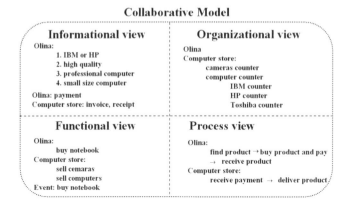

Figure 2. *Collaborative Model of Olina-Computer store example
in Mu Wenxin's PhD research*

Step 2: extraction of collaborative process model (one of the meta-models which cover collaboration situation framework). Deduced from the collaborative model, a collaborative process model, which contains more information than in the first BPMN restricted approach (about partners, message flows and sub-process) is extracted.

4. Conclusions

A main deliverable of the MISE project is a global solution to promote interoperability between industrial actors who intend to collaborate following MDA principles. MISE promotes an interoperability design tool that aims to deal with data exchange functionalities, service sharing and dynamic process orchestrations. The engineering is based on a four-step process:

– build collaborative network and collaborative process;

– transfer collaborative process model into PIM;

– gather technical information and transfer PIM to PSM;

– transfer PSM to target software system.

However, assumptions made at the business level, technical level and general approach during a first experiment are depicted and have been discussed. In order to solve all these problems, two PhD subjects have been started (Miss. Mu Wenxin and Mr. Nicolas Boissel-Dallier). Mu Wenxin's subject aims to improve business level work and build a collaborative model with different views. This subject has been introduced in this paper. The objective of Nicolas Boissel-Dallier's subject is improving business activities to technical services binding. Their research work will be performed with close interactions and using common business cases.

5. References

[1] Konstantas D, Bourrières JP, Léonard M, Boudjlida N, *Interoperability of Enterprise Software and Applications. I-ESA'05,* pp. v-vi. Springer, Geneva, Switzerland (2005)

[2] Vernadat F, "Interoperable enterprise systems: architecture and methods". Plenary lecture, *IFAC/INCOM Conference,* Saint-Etienne (2006)

[3] Morley C, Hugues J, Leblanc B, *UML pour l'analyse d'un système d'information.* 2nd edition, Dunod, France (2002)

[4] Bénaben F, Touzi J, Rajsiri V, Pingaud H, *Collaborative Information System Design. AIM 2006 Information Systems and Collaboration: State of the Art and Perspectives,* pp 281-296. GI-Edition, Lecture Notes in Informatics (2006)

[5] Aubert B, Dussart A, SI Inter-Organisationnels. CIRANO Bourgogne report (2002)

[6] Bénaben F, Pingaud H, "The MISE Project: A First Experience in Mediation Information System Engineering". *Information Systems: People, Organizations, Institutions, and Technologies.* 2010. p. 399-406

[7] Rajsiri V, Lorré JP, Bénaben F, Pingaud H, "Knowledge-based system for collaborative process specification". Special issue of *CII (Computers in Industry),* Elsevier (2009)

[8] Bénaben F, Touzi J, Rajsiri V, Lorré JP, Pingaud H, "Mediation Information System Design in a Collaborative SOA Context through a MDD Approach". *Proceedings of MDISIS'08 (Special workshop of CAISE'08).* Montpellier, France (2008)

[9] Touzi J, Bénaben F, Pingaud H, Lorré JP, "A Model-Driven approach for Collaborative Service-Oriented Architecture design". Special issue of *IJPE (International Journal of Production Economics),* Elsevier (2008)

[10] Truptil S, Bénaben F, Couget P, Lauras M, Chapurlat V, Pingaud H, "Interoperability of information systems in crisis management: Crisis modeling and metamodeling". *Proceeding of I-ESA 2008: Enterprise Interoperability III,* Berlin, Germany (2008)

Role of Semantic Web in the Changing Context of Enterprise Collaboration

N. Khilwani* — J. A. Harding*

* Wolfson School of Mechanical and Manufacturing Engineering
Loughborough University
Loughborough
UK

ABSTRACT. In order to compete with the global giants, enterprises are concentrating on their core competencies and collaborating with organizations that complement their skills and core activities. The current trend is to develop temporary alliances of independent enterprises, in which companies can come together to share skills, core competencies and resources. However, knowledge sharing and communication among multidiscipline companies is a complex and challenging problem. In a collaborative environment, the meaning of knowledge is drastically affected by the context in which it is viewed and interpreted; thus necessitating the treatment of structure as well as semantics of the data stored in enterprise repositories. Keeping the present market and technological scenario in mind, this research aims to propose tools and techniques that can enable companies to assimilate distributed information resources and achieve their business goals.

KEYWORDS: enterprise collaboratiration, virtual collaboration, semantic web, ontology, text mining

1. Introduction

The current global market is characterized by dramatic and often unanticipated changes. Enterprises are operating in an environment where markets frequently change, new technologies continually emerge and competition is fierce at the global scale. In order to compete with global giants, enterprises are concentrating on their core competences and collaborating with companies that compliment their skills and core activities. Enterprise collaboration is a challenging but worthwhile move for companies which can result in massive reductions of fixed costs, overheads and manpower and improve survival and growth opportunities. It entails interoperability of applications and data sources so that they can easily be shared by business processes and information system. Basically, the concept of enterprise collaboration started in early 1990s, when dominant firms extended their boundaries and developed relationships with small companies, customers and services. In an extended enterprise model, companies focused on their core competences and outsourced other business and technical activities to outside suppliers and other service providers. This model of extending an enterprise forced partner companies to compromise their independence and focus on business functions rather than on their fundamental competencies.

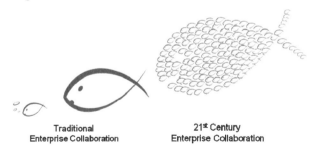

Traditional
Enterprise Collaboration

21ˢᵗ Century
Enterprise Collaboration

Figure 1. *Changing Context of Enterprise Collaboration [1]*

The negative aspect of the extended enterprise model led companies to adopt the concept of virtual collaboration. The concept of virtual collaboration is one of the most competitive approaches for enterprises wishing to enter the global market for collaboration whilst still maintaining their independence and autonomy [1]. This 21ˢᵗ century collaboration model is defined as a temporary alliance of independent enterprises in which companies come together to share skills, core competencies and resources in order to better respond to business opportunities. In such virtual collaboration, enterprises temporarily share competencies and resources to respond to business opportunities in a more collaborative rather than competitive manner. A self explanatory picture representing the two different models of enterprise collaboration is shown in Figure 1 [1].

In a virtual collaboration business, partners are integrated using information and communication technology, such as online service, Internet, etc. Information technology is reckoned as an essential strategy to store, publish, promote and share skills and abilities, and carry out collaboration efficiently. Advances in information technologies have strongly and consistently supported organizations to deliver *the right information to the right person at the right time*. The technology has weaved a pervasively networked world with millions of companies, billions of peoples and trillions of processes interconnected for handling the challenges of a network economy. Despite the increase in number of information entities (e.g. people, groups, organizations, etc) adopting such technological developments and joining the global market, little is known about companies with different organizational backgrounds, languages, customs, habits and locations.

In a collaborative environment, information resources are generally distributed throughout the collaboration pool, rather than being centralized. Amalgamating such information resources across multiple business functions and processes clearly has attractions since it reduces the potentials for errors caused by data duplication and the resulting inconsistencies. But diverging goals, objectives and operational disconnects among collaborating firms make this information sharing and communication more complex. The next generation enterprise community needs sets of interconnected data and semantic models to communicate and exchange their knowledge, without the current risk of misinterpretation. The aim of this research is *to explore how the latest technological advancements can usefully be exploited in enterprise collaborations to share and effectively utilize a full range of data, information and knowledge.*

2. Research idea

Although, information sharing and maintenance within a corporative environment has been considered for decades, it has always been an expensive and risky proposition [3]. It is only with the advent of web technology that information sharing has emerged as a technology area. Web technology has enabled firms to make their information available electronically so that users and application programmers can access and share their resources and expertise. Despite growing interest and efforts, this technology is still primitive in its functionality. Today's Web arranges the information syntactically, assuming it to be semantically homogenous which can commonly cause problems and misunderstandings. This downside means that most of the information must be interpreted by human before use, rather than machines. The availability of information that requires human interpretation does not necessarily solve the complex problem of getting *the right information to the right person at the right time*, since humans are not infallible and can also misinterpret particularly when ambiguities are present and quantities of information are high.

Information sharing and communication among multidisciplinary enterprises requires the treatment of structure as well as semantics of the data stored in those repositories. Collaborating partners often use different terminologies to describe the same meaning or alternatively the same terminology may be associated with different meanings. Such lack of clear semantic description of the meaning of contents in a particular domain has hampered the interoperability and shareability of information between collaborative firms. In order to handle this interoperability challenge of future organizations, it is necessary to make information explicit and machine interpretable. To overcome this problem, researchers are focusing on semantic web concepts and tools that enable computers to automatically process and understand the information.

The Semantic Web is a vision for extending current web technology in which information is annexed with a well defined meaning that enhances the interoperability of computers and people [2]. The primary benefit of this new vision of Tim Berners-Lee *et al.* is to represent the web resources in formalisms that both machines and humans can understand, thereby unleashing the potential for software agents to perform tasks on behalf of humans. The concept of the semantic web is, without any doubt, gaining attention in both industry and academia. The growing access to heterogenous and independent data repositories in enterprise collaboration is attracting a lot of research communities to identify methods for representing data in a way that it can be shared and processed automatically on the Semantic Web.

Keeping the present market and technological scenario in mind, this research aims to determine a platform that enables companies to achieve their potential through semantic web technology and assimilate distributed information resources [4].

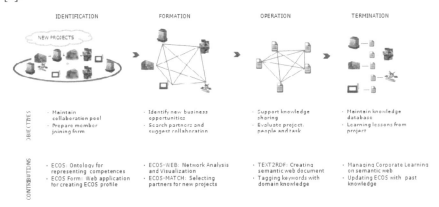

Figure 2. *Objectives and Contributions*

The idea is to provide explicit semantic descriptions to all information resources and encode them in an unambiguous and machine-understandable form. The purpose of this platform will be to share information among project teams and organizations in the context of a specific problem domain upon which action can be taken or advised.

3. Objective of research

Virtual collaborations are based on a perception that together partners can achieve some specific business goals that they could not undertake individually. The prime challenge of creating and operating a virtual collaboration is the selection and implementation of appropriate business partnerships and processes. Once the collaboration is achieved its efficiency is determined by the speed and accuracy with which information can be managed and exchanged among the business partners. Its construction consists of four stages:

– *Identification*: a stage where the partners wait for a business opportunity.

– *Formation*: when a collaboration is achieved to meet some business need – i.e. to carry out some project.

– *Operation*: in this phase each enterprise performs the specified task by using their core competencies and using relevant information from other collaborators.

– *Termination*: finally, the collaboration is disbanded in this phase.

This research aims to analyze the lifecycle of virtual collaboration, identify the tasks in each phase of collaboration and propose tools and techniques to facilitate those tasks. The objectives and contributions of this research are shown in Figure 2.

3.1. *Identification stage*

This is the stage where prospective companies are in pursuit of emerging business opportunities. Enterprises search for projects that can be handled individually or in collaboration with other companies. In order to develop a collaborative environment, a relatively stable network of potentially collaborating companies needs to be established to provide a basis for social relationships and trust among companies. The companies willing to develop such a network must publish information about their competences (knowledge that the enterprise is willing to make public) that they are able to offer in a collaboration.

In this research, *ecos* (Enterprise Competence Organization Schema) ontology is introduced to represent the published competences of enterprises (http://kmm.lboro.ac.uk/ontologies/ecos/). Ontology-based knowledge representation is a powerful scheme to model concepts and relationships that allows knowledge to be designed, shared and reused in a disciplined way [4]. *ecos* captures the domain knowledge and establishes common vocabularies which can be understood by systems as well as humans. It is used to capture, organize and publish enterprise competence under four fundamental domains i.e. general information, business details, specific information and business records and is further represented through an explicit ontology language (OWL) that can be interpreted by software as well as humans. A simple Web application, named *ecos* form, has been developed to create *ecos* cards and publish them on the web (http://www-staff.lboro.ac.uk/~mmnk/research/identification.html).

3.2. *Formation stage*

In this stage, enterprises develop a relatively stable network of partners for the collaboration. Such a network gives a basis for social relationships and trust among companies. In order to support collaboration, the new business opportunities must be identified and awareness created about the opportunities among the potential collaborating partners [5]. In this research, two services are developed for this purpose (http://www-staff.lboro.ac.uk/~mmnk/research/formation.html):

– *ecos-match*: analyze, process and categorize *ecos* profiles based on business opportunities.

– *ecos-web*: a toolkit to analyze, visualize and reason enterprise networks.

3.3. *Operation stage*

In a virtual collaboration, knowledge is distributed throughout the collaboration pool, rather than being centralized. Distributed knowledge means that no-one is capable of achieving the highest level goal(s) on his own; goal achievement becomes a team activity, where different enterprises share information for the achievement of goal(s). However, compared to single enterprises, knowledge sharing and communication among multidisciplinary teams is a notoriously challenging and complex problem [6]. Collaborating partners often use different terminologies to describe the same meaning or the same terminology is associated with different meaning. Such lack of semantic description about the meaning of contents in a particular domain hampers the interoperability and sharability of knowledge between collaborative firms.

Bearing in mind the present requirement, a specialized knowledge service is proposed in this research that gleans information from documents and converts it into a semantic web resource using RDF and RDF Schema. The proposed text mining tool, TEXT2RDF, provides explicit semantic descriptions to the enterprise documents and encodes them in an unambiguous and machine understandable format. The primary benefit of this new technique is to represent information resources in a manner that computers can understand and manipulate easily.

3.4. *Termination stage*

Finally, at this stage the collaborative project is finished and the network is disbanded. In this phase, the need is to gather experience from project members and utilize it in future projects. Although, the shared knowledge is unlikely to be needed in its shared format after termination, anything of future use should be retained by individual companies [7]. In this stage, the proposed TEXT2RDF tool is used to extract information from the text documents (e.g. project reviews, deliverables, etc.) and make users aware of it by updating the past knowledge database.

4. Conclusion

Enterprises regard their knowledge resources as a primary wealth and utilize it to contribute to the distinctive features of the company, since it can play a key role in enhancing organization performance. However to achieve and exploit the benefits potentially available from available knowledge, it is essential to store, update, share, promote and transfer its corporate memory efficiently. This research work aims to exploit the emerging semantic technologies e.g. ontology modeling and semantic web services to assimilate distributed information resources and exploit them to facilitate enterprise collaboration. A demonstration of this research work is avaialble online: http://www-staff.lboro.ac.uk/~mmnk/research/phd.html.

5. References

[1] Thompson K., *The Networked Enterprise: Competing the Future Through Virtual Enterprise Networks*, Meghan Kiffer, Tampa (2008).

[2] Berners-Lee T., Hendler J., "Publishing on the semantic web", *Nature 410*, 1023-24, (2001).

[3] Lai L.F., "A knowledge engineering approach to knowledge management", *Information Sciences*, vol. 177, pp. 4072-4094, 10/1 (2007).

[4] Khilwani N., Harding J.A., Choudhary A.K, *Semantic Web in Manufacturing*, vol. 223, no7, pp. 905-924, (2009).

[5] Huang N., Diao S., "Ontology based enterprise knowledge integration", Robotics and Computer Integrated Manufacturing, 2007.

[6] Huang C.C., Tseng T.L., Kusiak A., "XML-Based Modeling of Corporate Memory", *IEEE Transactions on Systems, Man, and Cybernetics: Part A*, vol. 35 (5), pp. 629-640, (2005).

[7] Dieng R., Corby O., Giboin A., Ribiere M., "Methods and Tools for Corporate Knowledge Management", International Journal of Human Computer Studies, vol. 51, No. 3, pp. 567-598, (Sept. 1999).

A Dynamic Knowledge Management Framework

B. A. Piorkowski* — J. X. Gao*

* Centre for Innovative Product Development
University of Greenwich
Chatham Maritime ME4 4TB
UK

ABSTRACT. Knowledge alone cannot achieve business results. People need to make decisions on how to act based on knowledge that is available. Face-to-face meetings (F2F) offer an opportunity to identify who within an organisation uses knowledge to shape the successful development of a product. The references to knowledge in conversations that take place at F2F meetings could be considered to be the most important to the current issues that are of value to a business. So far in the literature there has been no critical investigation of the contributions people make in a F2F meeting and how these discussions shapes the development of a product and the profitability of a business. Analysis of F2F meetings will therefore aid both personal and product development. The proposed Dynamic Knowledge Management Framework for integrated product development has been inspired from the work of Nonka (1994), Choi and Lee (2003) and Chua (2004) and is a combination of technological and cultural factors. The scope of the academic research project is to focus on codifying product development knowledge for interoperability within a Dynamic Knowledge Management Framework by profiling people's capability and competency through F2F meeting content analysis. This will involve assigning metadata to F2F meeting content so that is discoverable using a search engine. A personal profile gathered through F2F meetings that is semantically linked to interoperable Performance Development (PDR) and Product Life-cycle Management (PLM) systems will provide a method of ratifying knowledge against performance results as it is theorized that participants who have learnt the appropriate capabilities to a higher competency will have more valuable knowledge which is available to exploit and therefore the action they have taken should yield more profit for the company.

KEYWORDS: dynamic knowledge management, product development, performance review meeting

1. Introduction to product development knowledge and related issues

In the age before scribes, the printing press and computers, knowledge was passed on through verbal communication based on the storyteller's interpretation of past events. Societal advancement has meant that events can now be captured in a wide variety of media formats that form a body of knowledge which shapes future civilised progression. Nonaka (1994) theorized a dynamic spiral to create organisational knowledge depending on the direction of flow of information between people (informal – tacit) and multimedia (formal – explicit) however it would be wrong to assume that knowing is as useful as doing. Knowledge Management (KM) therefore should be closely linked to performance so that people can profit from the value of knowledge. The four different styles of KM grouped by Choi and Lee (2003) are "System-orientated", "People-orientated", "Dynamic" and "Passive". According to survey results, the "Dynamic" KM style which is a combination of technological and cultural factors is the style that yields the highest company performance. Technological factors of KM being infrastructure, content and interface services have been presented by Chua (2004) and are expanded later in this report to include cultural factors of people and motivation.

Mortality rates of New Product Development (NPD) projects is high with projects that are defined as being successful is only around 15% (Barczak *et al.*, 2009). Formal standard processes like the Performance Development Review (PDR) for people to reflect on and set personal learning objectives and the Product Lifecycle Management (PLM) process are designed to link the actions and decisions people make to the success of NPD and the profitability of the company. PLM is a systematic method whereby only products that have met the prearranged project criteria may progress with appropriate funding. This is discussed and decided at F2F review meetings. The PDR process is where the people in the company should be motivated to achieve set goals. The competency of people capability could influence NPD success which seems like common sense but there has been no direct link between the two established in previous work. People capability in an engineering business context has been presented in four main points being strategic, functional and project capability all influencing people capability (Bredin, 2008). Decisions are made by people with an element of risk due to the lack of time available because time costs money and the wrong decision can not only be bad for short term profitability but may also have an adverse non-financial impact, e.g. reputational.

So far in the literature, the journey that people take in NPD and how knowledge influences the problem solving and decision-making has not been investigated. F2F meetings offer an opportunity to identify who within an organization uses knowledge to shape the successful development of a product. The references to knowledge in conversations that take place at F2F meetings could be considered to be the most important to the current issues that are of value to a business. Within large organizations there is existing enterprise software and applications that hold

PLM and PDR content. So far, there has been no critical investigation of the contributions people make in a F2F meeting and how these discussions shape the development of a product and the profitability of a business. Analysis of F2F meetings will therefore aid both personal and product development. It would be useful for organizations to have interoperable F2F, PLM and PDR systems embedded into the working culture so that there is a clear and common understanding between the people in the company and the machines that aid the people to make important decisions on how to act in the pursuit of excellence.

The aim of the investigation in progress therefore is to evaluate Dynamic knowledge generation in face-to-face meetings to inform profitable product development in a collaborative engineering context.

2. Codifying product development knowledge in F2F meetings

Knowledge alone cannot achieve business results, people need to take action and apply this knowledge to develop products and keep a business profitable. Identification and motivation of talented people in an organization has been facilitated with reward and recognition schemes which have matured into knowledge capture interfaces linked to the company infrastructure (Cummings, 2004). It has been reported by Cummings (2004) that future research should examine different measures of knowledge content exchanges and networks, as well as better metrics for capturing knowledge content such as real-time surveillance techniques. Performance analysis of the people, their contribution to knowledge and their contribution to company profits will provide a map of the current value of organisational knowledge. It will also inform potential gaps in knowledge which could impact future product and business performance.

Life-log media capture technology has featured in the literature (Kim *et al.*, 2008). Logging the life of a face-to-face (F2F) meeting room where many people share stories and make decisions to impact on the profitability of a business could provide a rich source of media content that opens up hidden knowledge that was previously only made available to a select few behind closed doors. This means that there are sensitivity issues when planning interoperability between F2F, PLM and PDR systems including adherence to acts of parliament such as the Official Secrets Act (1989), Data Protection Act (1998) and Export Control Act (2002).

Engaging participant volunteers to tell stories of their experiences in a digitally recorded F2F meeting scenario will allow for a rich multimedia user profile which can be linked to the existing and or future knowledge content held in the company infrastructure. This means that there would be opportunity for others to connect to the storyteller F2F so that they can benefit from their peer's knowledge before embarking on their own action toward product development.

Theorem 1. Participants who have learnt the appropriate capabilities to a higher competency will have more valuable knowledge which is available to exploit and therefore the action they have taken should yield more profit for the company.

There are aids available to assist a human post-processor codifying meeting (video and audio) content including computer-assisted qualitative data analysis software (CAQDAS). CAQDAS is widely applied in academia whereby researchers with a theory and explanatory models use the computer application to answer questions by gathering evidence from a number of different media sources (Bringer *et al.*, 2006). Codified people profiles made available in the company infrastructure linked to existing PDR and PLM enterprise software applications is an interoperability challenge that will require a large community of users motivated to assign and continuously improve meta-data tags to F2F meeting content. Codification means tagging content with keyword text against predefined classification ontology. User-generated tagging to a structured meta-data standard will allow pertinent sections of the meeting to be played back using a search engine with matching keywords or through ontological navigation. Previously uncaptured, unstructured conversation will be discoverable online by using life-log type technology so that experts and decision makers can be identified for future engagement. It will also provide an audit trail to examine the link between knowledge and performance. It is the intention that a Dynamic KM Framework will evolve from the research project and a prototype tool will be evaluated. The benefit this will bring to industry is a method to leverage yesterday's experience to sell and deliver tomorrow's solutions today.

3. Proposed dynamic knowledge management framework

The proposed Dynamic Knowledge Management (KM) Framework for integrated product development has been inspired from the work of Nonka (1994), Choi and Lee (2003) and Chua (2004) and is a combination of technological and cultural factors.

The technological factors of the proposed framework include restricted access to the company internal infrastructure. The infrastructure allows the storage and connectivity of content which pertains to the company's people, products and processes. The references to knowledge in conversations that take place at F2F meetings could be considered to be the most important to the current issues that are of value to a business. This is because the key people within an organization are required to attend Product Lifecycle Management (PLM) review meetings to improve the sale and delivery of products. This means that the knowledge that they hold is vital to the success of the business. Another technological factor is interface services. The proposed Dynamic KM Framework has two main interfaces. One is the human computer interface to search both the internal (intranet, databases, enterprise software) and external infrastructure (Internet). This interface also provides access control and personalized presentation of content depending on the end-users viewing rights. The second interface is the human to human interface between people at face-to-face (F2F) meetings. Both of these interfaces rely on a common understanding for smooth communication however it is important not to ignore conflict as this can lead to innovation. F2F meetings are a flexible and adaptable way of finding things out. F2F meetings give deep understanding of participants and their internal interpretation of the world as they see it. Semi-structured F2F meetings have predefined questions and set boundaries but there is flexibility so that the order of questions may be changed (and questions omitted) based on what is appropriate. It is the intention to capture F2F meeting content (video and audio) data through a Polycom CX5000 table-mounted 360° web camera (Polycom, Slough UK) with PC and software. The post-processing of the data for this project can be achieved by using computer-assisted qualitative data analysis software (NVivo8, QSR, Victoria, Australia) which allows users to codify the data so that is compatible with the company meta-data policy on upload and discoverable within the company Share Point infrastructure (Microsoft, Reading, UK) using the enterprise search engine. Personalized viewing rights will be applied which will be determined by cross-referencing individual user profiles against the meta-data associated to the content with the search engine browser filtering out necessary sections. Once the F2F meeting content is uploaded into Share Point, crowd-based organic knowledge generation is anticipated to grow from multiple users adding text based comments and suggestions on the webpage.

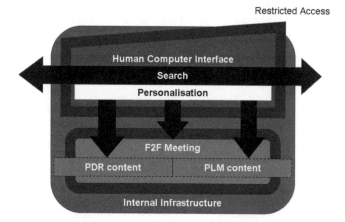

Figure 1. *Proposed Dynamic KM Framework*

The framework depends on motivated people to actively seek, share and learn (Figure 1). People and motivation are therefore the cultural factors of the framework. If people do not participate by accessing the interface services or are not motivated to improve product profitability then the framework is useless. When people contribute to the content then they are making their existing knowledge available for re-use to be attempted. If people spot opportunities to improve on current gaps then they are generating new knowledge. Experts will be identified from attendance of F2F meetings and they should then be made available to support others in improving their capability and competency which may lead to some form of knowledge transfer or shared experience between the parties. As a greater number of people become more competent in the required capabilities then there should be more opportunities for business successes.

4. Conclusion

The scope of the academic research project is to focus on codifying product development knowledge for interoperability within a Dynamic Knowledge Management Framework by profiling people's capability and competency through face-to-face (F2F) meeting content analysis. This will involve assigning meta-data to F2F meeting content so that is discoverable using a search engine. There are personal, commercial, security and legal sensitivity issues involved which means that care and attention will be taken to apply personalized access filters to the content. A personal profile gathered through F2F meetings that is semantically linked to interoperable PDR and PLM systems will provide a method of ratifying knowledge against performance results as it is theorized that participants who have learnt the appropriate capabilities to a higher competency will have more valuable knowledge which is available to exploit and therefore the action they have taken should yield more profit for the company.

5. Acknowledgements

This project is sponsored by EPSRC through BAE Systems. The public funding was won by Clive Simmonds and Nick Martin from BAE Systems and the researchers are deeply grateful to Nick, Clive and others for the support in making this project possible

6. References

(1989) The Official Secrets Act 1889 (52 & 53 Vict. c. 52), UK.

(1998) Data Protection Act 1998, UK.

(2002) Export Control Act 2002, UK.

Barczak, G., Griffin, A. & Kahn, K. B. (2009) "PERSPECTIVE: Trends and Drivers of Success in NPD Practices: Results of the 2003 PDMA Best Practices Study". *Journal of Product Innovation Management,* 26, 3–23.

Bredin, K. (2008) "People capability of project-based organisations: A conceptual framework". *International Journal of Project Management,* 26, 566-576.

Bringer, J. D., Johnston, L. H. & Brackenridge, C. H. (2006) "Using Computer-Assisted Qualitative Data Analysis Software to Develop a Grounded Theory Project". *Field Methods,* 18, 245-266.

Choi, B. & Lee, H. (2003) "An empirical investigation of KM styles and their effect on corporate performance". *Information & Management,* 40, 403-417.

Chua, A. (2004) "Knowledge management system architecture: a bridge between KM consultants and technologists". *International Journal of Information Management,* 24, 87-98.

Cummings, J. N. (2004) "Work Groups, Structural Diversity, and Knowledge Sharing in a Global Organization". *Management Science,* 50, 352–364.

Kim, I.-J., Ahn, S. C., Ko, H. & Kim, H.-G. (2008) "Automatic Lifelog media annotation based on heterogenous sensor fusion". *Multisensor Fusion and Integration for Intelligent Systems.* Seoul, IEEE.

Nonaka, I. (1994) "A Dynamic Theory of Organizational Knowledge Creation". *Organization Science,* 5, 14-37.

Author Index